Susman & Chambers, American History

Selected Reading Lists and Course
Outlines from American Colleges
and Universities

American History
Vol. III: Selected Topics in
Twentieth Century History

edited by Warren Susman and John Chambers
Rutgers University

MARKUS WIENER PUBLISHING, INC.

216065

Second Printing 1986
© 1983 by Markus Wiener Publishing, Inc.

ISBN 0-910129-06-1
Library of Congress Card No. 83-061362
Printed in America

TABLE OF CONTENTS

VOLUME III

Documents have been reproduced from the originals as submitted.

SEE PAGE 182 FOR TABLE OF CONTENTS

OF VOLUME I, VOLUME II AND WOMEN'S HISTORY

STANFORD UNIVERSITY

History 165c
Spring Quarter, 1982-83
David M. Kennedy

THE UNITED STATES IN THE TWENTIETH CENTURY

This course seeks to provide students with a basic understanding
of the major political, economic, social, and diplomatic issues
facing the United States from the end of the nineteenth century
to the present.

Lectures will normally be on Monday, Tuesday, and Wednesday
mornings at 9:00. We will occasionally meet also on Thursdays.
PLEASE NOTE that there will be NO CLASS on Wednesday, April 6.

The lectures will proceed according to the following schedule.
You will get more out of the lectures if you complete the
relevant reading assignments BEFORE the indicated dates.

Week of:

March 28: The nineteenth-century background -- the economy,
ideology, and law.

April 4: The era of progressive reform
    Reading: John W. Chambers, The Tyranny of Change

April 11: The origins of modern American foreign policy
    Reading: David M. Kennedy, Over Here: The First World War
             and American Society

April 18: The 1920s, the Great Depression, and the New Deal
    Reading: William Leuchtenburg, Franklin D. Roosevelt and the
             New Deal

April 25: World War II -
    Reading: John Morton Blum, V Was for Victory: Politics and
             American Culture during World War II

May 2: The Cold War
    Reading: John L. Gaddis, Strategies of Containment: A
             Critical Appraisal of Postwar American National
             Security Policy

May 9: Minorities in modern America
    Reading: Harvard Sitkoff, The Struggle for Black Equality,
             1954-1980

May 16: The 1960s and Vietnam
    Reading: David Harris, Dreams Die Hard: Three Men's Journey
             through the Sixties

1

May 23: Contemporary America in historical perspective
        Reading: William Chafe, The American Woman in the 20th
                 Century: Her Changing Political, Social, and
                 Economic Role, 1920-1970

All of the above titles are available for purchase at the Stanford
Bookstore. David Harris, Dreams Die Hard may arrive after the
beginning of the quarter.

EXAMS

There will be an optional mid-term examination (in take-home
format) during the week of April 25. I strongly urge you to take
the mid-term exam, so that you may benefit from the reader's
comments and familiarize yourself with the type of questions and
format that you will encounter on the final examination.

PASS-NO CREDIT OPTION

The pass-no credit option is available, under the usual University
guidelines.

INCOMPLETES

Incompletes will be considered only on presentation of convincing
evidence of medical disability.

HONORS DISCUSSION SECTION

History graduate student Jim Campbell will offer an "Honors"
discussion section in this course. Weekly meetings will provide
those who participate the opportunity to deepen their
understanding of the course material, and to develop critical and
analytical skills through discussion. Participation in the
discussion section is entirely voluntary, but once you have
elected to participate, regular attendance will be expected.

PAPER

This course requires all students to write a paper of
approximately 2,000-3,000 words (8-10 double-spaced, typed
pages). The paper must be based on primary sources, rather than
on accounts by other historians. Examples of primary sources are
contemporary newspapers, magazines, government documents,
autobiographies, diaries, memoirs, letters -- in general, any
document t6hat is contemporary with the problem under
investigation and that is itself direct evidence for a particular
argument or position. The already-processed interpretation of
another writer is not a primary source.

Papers will be due on Tuesday, May 31. The attached material
concerning historical research and writing should guide you into
this project. Please see Jim Campbell about any problems.

NOTE: A one-page typed prospectus of your paper is due on
Monday, April 18. Your prospectus should give the title of your
proposed paper, a brief outline of the questions to be examined,
and a preliminary list of the primary sources to be used.

OFFICE HOURS

Jim Campbell will hold regular weekly office hours, at a time
and place to be announced. I will not have regular office hours,
but you can make an appointment to see me by calling 497-9784.

History 165c: lecture schedule

Spring Quarter, 1983

Week of March 28:   T(29): Late 19th-century economy
  (Progressivism)   W(30): Conservative social thought
                       Th(31): The problem of progressivism

Week of April 4:   M(4): Theodore Roosevelt
  (Progressivism)   T(5): Conservation as a case study
                       W(6): OPEN ? (travel to OAH)

Week of April 11:   M(11): Woodrow Wilson, domestic
  (foreign pol.)   T(12): Spanish-American War
                       W(13): Roosevelt and foreign policy
                       Th(14): World War I, foreign policy

Week of April 18:   M(18): World War I, international consequences
  (WWI)   T(19): Immigration
                       W(20): Blacks in early 20th century
                       Th(21): World War I, domestic

Week of April 25:   M(25): The 1920s
  (1920s)   T(26): The Great Depression
                       W(27): Herbert Hoover
                       Th(28): OPEN

Week of May 2:   M(2): The New Deal: approaches
  (New Deal)   T(3): The New Deal: legacy
                       W(4): Isolationism in the 1930s
                       Th(5): OPEN

Week of May 9:   M(9): World War II: military and diplomatic
  (WWII)   T(10): World War II: domestic
                       W(11): Political economy of the post-war period
                       Th(12): OPEN

Week of May 16:   M(16): The atomic bomb
  (Cold War)   T(17): FILM ON THE ATOMIC BOMB
                       W(18): Cold War
                       Th(19): Cold War, II

Week of May 23:   M(23): McCarthyism
  (post-war)   T(24): Post-WWII intellectuals
                       W(25): Women in modern America
                       Th(26): Blacks and Civil Rights

Week of May 30:   M(30): MEMORIAL DAY HOLIDAY
  (end)   T(31): conclusion

HISTORY 165C FINAL EXAM
David M. Kennedy
May 31-June 6, 1983

This take-home exam is due in the History Department office no
later than 12:00 noon, Monday, June 6, 1983. Please note that all
the Honor Code regulations pertinent to take-home exams apply.
You may consult your notes and books, but should not discuss the
course material with anyone other than the teaching assistant or
the instructor during the entire 6-day examination period.

Please answer two (2) of the following questions. Your answer to
each should not exceed 1250 words -- approximately 5 double-
spaced typed pages. This means that your total exam should not
exceed 2500 words, or about 10 double-spaced typed pages.

I. "In the last eight decades the United States has emerged from
an 18th-century system of weak national government into a modern
system of massive governmental presence in many areas of society.
Mainstream ideology, once deeply anti-statist, now holds that the
state is virtuous. The national government has not only grown
big; it has adopted policies whose purpose has been to underwrite
most of the other large institutions, so that we now have
socialism for the organized and capitalism for the unorganized.
So different is this modern system from the system preceding
it that it deserves to be called The Second Republic."

Comment critically on this statement. How accurate is it? To the
extent that it is an accurate description of reality, what forces
and/or events have most notably shaped the developments here
described? What, for example, has been the role of "reform"
movements such as progressivism and the New Deal? Of traumatic
events like World Wars I and II and the Great Depression? Of
ideology?

II. In what ways were Jimmy Carter's difficulties in foreign
policy reflective of unresolved problems in American foreign
policy in the entire Cold War era -- or, indeed, in the entire
twentieth century? Be specific in describing Carter's
difficulties, and in identifying their historical antecedents.

III. Did the feminist movement succeed?
     In answering this question, you may want to consider the
movement's goals, its ideology, its internal divisions, and its
opposition. Also, what is an appropriate definition of "success"
in this case? What factors have most contributed to the
movement's progress? What has been the role of government in
this process?

[Please Note: Alternatively, you may address the same set of
issues using the civil rights movement as your case in point; if
you really want to go for broke, you might try comparing the two
movements with respect to the above questions -- a high-risk,
high-reward choice.]

5

<u>Some</u> <u>Notes</u> on <u>the</u> <u>Written</u> Assignment for 165C:

It is sometimes forgotten that history is a creative project as much as it is a body of knowledge to be read and discussed. Just as you would not confuse the enjoyment of listening to music with the fun of playing an instrument yourself, history is something that one can <u>do</u> as well as read about. One of the objects of this course is to introduce students to this form of creative activity by requiring that everyone write a small piece of history about some topic in twentieth-century American life.

You should keep several things in mind as you start on this assignment. First, it is important to understand what kinds of materials provide the basis for writing history. All sorts of written documents are possible—newspapers, magazines, Senate or House committee hearing transcripts, personal letters, memoirs, minutes of an organization's meetings, the speeches of a political figure, the transcript of a trial, federal or state census reports—the only stipulation is that these documents, known as primary sources, must date from the time under study. Thus, a history book written after the event in which you are interested is <u>not</u> a document that dates from the period in question. It is someone else's interpretation of the event, someone else's history. You might be interested in such a history book, a secondary source, for the sake of comparison or to provide background for you own research topic; but primary sources should form the principal basis for your own work. For example, if you want to investigate the 1925 Scopes "Monkey" trial in which attorney Clarence Darrow opposed William Jennings Bryan, you might study the transcript of the trial, local Tennessee newspapers, or national press accounts (to discover attitudes toward the trial in different parts of the country). Or, valuable information might be found in the memoirs of Bryan or Darrow, but you should ot base your work principally on such a secondary source as Ray Ginger's SIX DAYS OR FOREVER? TENNESSEE v. JOHN THOMAS SCOPES, published in 1958.

Second, there are many kinds of history and much leeway in choosing subject matter. For instance, you may wish to write about an idea (perhaps isolationism in the 1930s), the social history of a group (black migration from the South to Chicago during World War I), or the political history of a movement (i.e., Huey Long's challenge to the New Deal). Other topics might be the diplomatic history of the United States government for a particular period (i.e., the Roosevelt Administration's policy toward Jewish refugees from Nazi Germany) or the economic history of a region (i.e., the development of the Southwest since World War II.)

Included below is a list of possible topics. Many of them will not be familiar to you, especially at the beginning of the course. You can begin your exploration of the topic either in the required reading for the course or any recent textbook concerning twentieth-century U.S. history. Probably the most comprehensive such textbook is Arthur S. Link, AMERICAN EPOCH. THE HARVARD GUIDE TO AMERICAN HISTORY, THE ENCYCLOPEDIA OF AMERICAN HISTORY, edited by Richard B. Morris, and THE DICTIONARY OF AMERICAN BIOGRAPHY are sources worth consulting when searching for a topic and specific information.

Ask for assistance from the reference librarians in Meyer and Green Libraries.
Narrowing your topic and developing an outline will be key parts of writing
your paper. In any event, here are sample topics:

    Japanese exclusion, 1900, 1907-08
    Immigration literacy tests, 1896, 1913, 1915, and 1917
    Immigration restriction, 1924
    Homestead Massacre, 1892
    Pullman Strike, 1894 (or any other major strike)
    Child labor legislation, 1916 and 1919
    Tax legislation (fight over the income tax, 1894-1913; Revenue Act of
        1918; New Deal Revenue Acts; tax reforms under Kennedy)
    A presidential campaign, 1890-1980
    Tariff legislation
    Regulatory legislation: Federal Trade Commission, 1914; Hepburn Act,
        1906, Securities and Exchange Commission, 1934
    Sherman Antitrust Act, 1890; Clayton Antritrust, 1914
    Coxey's Army, 1894
    Panic of 1893
    Conservation movement in the Progressive Era or during the New Deal
    Ballinger-Pinchot controversy
    Preparedness movement, 1914-17 or 1939-41
    Decision to annex the Philippines or Hawaii
    Theodore Roosevelt and the Panama Canal
    America in WW I (some aspect of diplomacy, military history, war-time
        legislation, or social events in the period)
    Espionage Act, 1917
    Sedition Act, 1918
    Prohibition (choose a particular state, for instance)
    The Versailles Treaty
    The Scopes Trial - 1925
    The Ku Klux Klan in the 1920s
    The Bonus Army, 1932
    The Crash of 1929
    Philanthropy--Carnegie, Rockefeller, Ford
    The Nineteenth Amendment (Women Suffrage)
    An important Supreme Court Case (Reagan v. Farmer's Loan and Trust, 1894;
        Muller v. Oregon, 1908; Plessy v. Ferguson, 1896; Brown v. Board of
        Education, 1954; Miranda; Bakke)
    The reform movement in a given city in the Progressive Era
    The Lusitania incident
    German-American relations in WW I
    The controversy over foreign language instruction in the schools during
        the late 19th century (in given state or locality)
    The beginning of the NAACP
    Marcus Garvey
    W.E.B. DuBois and World War I
    Hiram Johnson
    Frederick Winslow Taylor
    Margaret Sanger
    Charlotte Perkins Gilman
    Agricultural policies under a certain president
    Major New Deal legislation
    The Stimson doctrine
    The Panay incident

America and the Munich crisis (1938)
America First Movement
The court-packing controversy
Wendell Willkie
Thomas Dewey
Anti-Japanese sentiment in California after Pearl Harbor; forced
    evacuation of Japanese
Attitudes toward Russia or England during WW II
The Yalta Conference (or Potsdam)
Labor in World War II
Popular reaction to Roosevelt's death (or the Kennedy brothers or Martin
    Luther King)
Debate on the Truman Doctrine, the Marshall Plan
Beginnings of NATO
Reactions to the Fall of China
The Progressive Party, 1948
Alger Hiss
Robert Oppenheimer
Julius and Ethel Rosenberg
The Point IV Program
The early political career of Richard Nixon
Taft-Hartley Act
Civil Rights Act of 1957 or 1964
The National Defense Act of 1958
The G.I. Bill after the Korean War or WW II
Suez invasion of 1956
U-2 incident of 1960
The Cuban Missile Crisis
Debate on Medicare
HUAC
Vietnam--why it happened (or Cambodia)
The Equal Rights Amendment
Controversy over abortion
Proposition 13
Demographic changes
Watergate
The U.S. and the Middle East
Desegregation efforts
Concern for human rights
The Moral Majority

Thomas S. Hines

History 6C

Spring Quarter, 1980
Young Hall 2276
MW, 12:00

"History of the American Peoples: The Twentieth Century"

COURSE SYLLABUS

History 6C is the third part of the three-quarter introductory course in United States history. Its title "History of the American Peoples" reflects its emphasis on social and cultural matters, though it also explores the inextricably connected political, economic, and diplomatic developments. The coordinating professor, Thomas Hines, will deliver two 50-minute lectures each week. TAs, in charge of directing the weekly two-hour discussion sections, are Michael Fitzgerald, Judy Kutulas, Dan Lund, Tanis Thorne, and David Waterhouse.

READINGS

The basic "texts" are: (a) The National Experience: A History of the United States Since 1865, by John Blum, Edmund Morgan, et al., and Three Generations in Twentieth Century America: Family, Community, and Nation, by John G. Clark, David M. Katzman, Richard D. McKinzie and Theodore A. Wilson. The first provides a good outline of the political, economic, social, cultural, and diplomatic history of twentieth century America. The second focuses on some twelve American families of widely differing social, cultural, economic, political, ethnic, ecological, and geographic identities. How and why the authors chose these particular representative families is discussed in the book's preface and various appendicies. Supplementing the texts are four additional books, all available in paperback at the UCLA Student Store:

1. Jane Addams, Twenty Years at Hull House

2. Sinclair Lewis, Babbitt

3. Malcolm X and Alex Haley, The Autobiography of Malcolm X

4. Studs Terkel, Division Street: America

All four volumes are different types of primary historical documents. (1) and (3) are both autobiographies, (1) by a white, upper middle class female social worker and philosopher; (3) by a black, male activist/philosopher, as told to a gifted black journalist. (2) is a novel and will allow us to deal with the question of "fiction" as historical document. (4) is a classic example of the "oral history" method.

The four volumes span the twentieth century and will be read in a generally chronological order. (1) provides an important 19th century prelude to the "reform era" in the early 20th century. (2) deals brilliantly with most of the major social and cultural issues of the 1920s, with implications for other periods. (3) moves through the '30s, '40s and '50s to a dramatic climax in the 1960s. (4) is a series of interviews of people in the 1960s, but of sufficiently different age groups to furnish interesting retrospective observations on earlier decades and suggest hopes, needs, goals, and "predictions" of the future.

All four deal (with varying degrees of directness) with different social, economic, ethnic, geographic, ideological, and gender groupings. No one book or group of books on this or any list is perfect for all needs, but given the constraints of time and focus, these seemed the best complements to a) the texts and b) the lectures. They are all well written and should be engaging to most students in the course.

Equivalent to the four documentary readings will be a showing of the film: "The Grapes of Wrath" (Melnitz 1409 on 7 May at 5:30) which focuses on the 1930s. Two shorter films will screen at 5:30 Thursday, 22 May, in Young 2250 on ethnic groups in Los Angeles: "The Exiles" (a study of "urban Indians") and "Sam: the Story of a Japanese Gardener". There will, at the same time, also be an introductory film: "Landscape with Angels: A History of Los Angeles."

To supplement the assigned readings (for students who need more detailed information) the following can be found on reserve:

> Richard B. Morris, editor, Encyclopedia of American History
>
> Wayne Andrews, editor, Concise Dictionary of American History
>
> Kenneth Boulding, The Image: Knowledge in Life and Society

READING SCHEDULE

Students should have completed the following readings by the beginning of the week in question:

WEEK OF:	READING:
31 March	Chapters 1 and 2 of Kenneth Boulding, The Image: Knowledge in Life and Society (multiple copies on reserve). Discuss syllabus and course plan in sections.
7 April	Three Generations, chapter 1; National Experience, chapters 23-24.
14 April	Addams, Twenty Years at Hull House.
21 April	Three Generations, chapter 5; National Experience, chapter 25.
29 April	Lewis, Babbitt.
5 May	National Experience, chapters 26-27; see film "Grapes of Wrath".
12 May	National Experience, chapters 28-30; Three Generations, chapter 10. (Complete and turn in papers.)
19 May	National Experience, chapter 31; Autobiography of Malcolm X; see films, "The Exiles" and "Sam".
26 May	National Experience, chapter 32; Terkel, Division Street: America.
2 June	National Experience, chapter 33 and Epilogue.

FINAL EXAM: Tuesday, 10 June, 11:30-2:30 (Young 2276).

LECTURES

There will be two lectures a week most of which will be visually and aurally illustrated with slides and music. They will be organized topically within a general chronological framework, touching and ty ing together the readings, but also attempting at times to go beyond them and to introduce students to ideas, problems, and possibilities that they might not otherwise get in readings or discussion sections. The lectures will not be "biographical" in the traditional sense, but they will be based upon or focused around the life experiences and contributions of a significant individual or group of individuals. The individual experiences will be used as a springboard for getting at important issues, movements, ideas and institutions. As opposed to the relatively "anonymous" twelve families of the text, the lectures will focus on the experiences of better known Americans.

(1)   The "Typical" American and the Search for the "National Character"

(2)   Abraham Cahan and the New American Immigrant

(3)   Robert LaFollette and American Liberal Reform

(4)   W. E. B. DuBois and the Organization of Black America

(5)   Henry Ford and the American Automobile

(6)   D. W. Griffith and the American Film

(7)   Frank Lloyd Wright and the New American Architecture

(8)   Sinclair Lewis: The Novelist as Social Observer

(9)   Walker Evans and Dorothea Lange: Photographing the "American Experience"

(10) Woody Guthrie and the Great Depression

(11) Henry Wallace, The New Deal and the American Progressive Tradition

(12) Joseph McCarthy and the Cold War Syndrome

(13) Allen Ginsburg and the "Beat Generation"

(14) Betty Friedan and the Dilemmas of American Feminism

(15) Lt. Calley, Captain Levy and the Vietnam Debacle

(16) Andy Warhol and Roy Liechtenstein: The 'Pop' Artist as Social Observer

(17) Who Speaks For the Seventies?

Topic (2) will deal with "old" and "new" immigration and will relate to Addams' Hull House. (3) will treat the "Progressive Era" and touch, from a different perspective, some of the issues also dealt with in Addams. (4) will concern Black Americans in the early 20th century, for which Malcolm X will serve as a mid-century complement. (5) will deal with Big Business, Nativism/Racism, philanthropy, and the automobile, with emphasis on the latter's effects on American society. (6) through (10) will treat issues and achievements in American cultural history, sweeping over several decades and illuminating in various ways the American "character" and environment. (10) will use the music, lyrics, and life-trek of this "folk" singer to explore the Depression of the 1930s. (11) will follow the "New Deal" of the '30s and the post-war Truman Era through the experience of a man whose "leftish" commitments stopped him just short of actually reaching the Presidency. (12) will explore the Cold War Mentality, with retrospective flashbacks to the "Red Scare" of the '20s. (13) will analyze the development of a new "sensibility" in the post-war epoch, especially among members of the younger generation.

11

(14) will use the experience of one of the leaders of the Woman's Movement as a base for assessing the meaning of twentieth century American feminism. (15) will assess the Vietnam tangle, with a look at one who "obeyed orders" at My Lai and another who went to prison for failure to comply. (16) will look at American values and mores in the 1960s through the work of the 'Pop' painters and sculptors.

PAPERS, EXAMINATIONS, DISCUSSION SECTIONS AND GRADES

The final will be a comprehensive three-hour essay examination of the material covered in readings, lectures, and discussions. Specific suggestions for preparation will be made throughout the course, particularly in the final week of review.

A short paper (approx. 5-10 typewritten pages) on the history of the student's own family and life experiences will take the place of a mid-term exam and will be due no later than the seventh week of class. Papers will be based upon students' own memories, interviews with family members, and examination of family records. Suggestive models are provided in Three Generations, to which students should compare their own family histories. Specific and more detailed instructions and suggestions will be given after the course begins. If students find they are absolutely unable (either for personal or logistical reasons) to write on themselves and their own families, an alternate topic may be arranged in consultation with TAs, though all are strongly encouraged to write on the assigned topic.

The weekly two-hour discussion sections coordinated by a graduate teaching assistant will be of a relatively informal nature, during which students may pose questions and discuss issues raised in readings and lectures and obtain counseling on preparing for the paper and exam.

Completion of all assigned readings and attendance at all class meetings and discussion sections is essential. The final exam, covering material from the whole course, will count approximately ½ of the final grade. The paper will count approximately ¼ and the student's performance in and contribution to discussions will also count approximately ¼. Methods of grading will be explained in course meetings.

GENERAL INFORMATION

"Incompletes will be given only in extreme emergencies. No exams can be given sooner than the time assigned in the course schedule. Because of the frequently "visual" nature of the Lectures, tape recorders will not be allowed. The same applies to the so-called published "class notes," which will not be available. Students should consider class notes a personal intellectual responsibility and should not rely on any one else's "canned" interpretation of the course. Hines' office hours are Wednesdays 3:00-5:00 and by appointment, Bunche Hall 5280. TAs will announce office hours at the first discussion section.

Students should remember that each of the various aspects of the course discussed above (readings, lectures, discussions, papers, exams) are in themselves only fragments and will remain fragments unless they, the students, put them together into an integrated whole. The professor giving lectures and organizing the course and the TAs coordinating discussion sections will assist in this integration whenever and however possible, but the students, after all, are the only ones who do it all, who participate in every single aspect of the course, and who are ultimately the most responsible for making it "work."

12

TOWARD A DEFINITION AND UNDERSTANDING OF HISTORY

If history is the reconstruction of the past, based upon surviving documents, and if the documents are records of (usually someone's) past perceptions of reality, then history could be characterized as our perceptions of other people's perceptions as recorded in surviving documents.

The word History is sometimes used as a synonym for the past itself, ("the sum total of human activity") but it seems more logical and useful to call the past simply "the past" and to define the term "history" as the study and reconstruction of the past. George Washington was then not a "maker" of history, but a figure of history. The historian, rather, is the maker of history -- the person who selects, organizes, and interprets the records with careful and "controlled imagination" and presents the findings and insights in a meaningful and effective verbal or literary form.

We might say that history is all we know about everything people have done or thought, or hoped, or felt -- the record and interpretation of all that has occurred within the realm of human consciousness.

History is, among other things, the study of change, of how and why people change, and what they have been despite all change.

There are almost as many reasons for studying history as there are people who study it. The most practical, immediate justification is that of seeking and establishing continuity, of getting to the beginning and earlier chapters of the story that we are now experiencing briefly in our own lives. This approach of "everything leading grandly to the present moment", of looking at history with an eye toward better understanding the present, is, of course, generally valid, but it is only one way of looking at things. There is a slightly different approach that would justify the study of history -- not so much for the light it throws on the present as for the light it throws on the age-old "human predicament" in general -- on what William Faulkner has called "the tragedy and comedy of being alive."

All of our lives will be short and limited in time. Most of our lives will be limited in space. And in fact when our lives end, we will have experienced relatively little in an actual or immediate sense.

But by studying history -- ' in all its forms, by touching intellectually other times, other places, other lives, other ideas (not in so much the sense of escaping our own time but rather transcending and enlarging it) we can extend, if not prolong, our lives -- both horizontally into space -- and vertically back into time.

Several themes and issues will pervade this course and should be considered at every step of the way: 1) the general and more abstract questions (for the lone individual or for the larger society) of "Liberty and/vs. Order" and "Freedom and/vs. Equality" and 2) the meaning for all Americans of the phrases: "Quality of Life" and "Pursuit of Happiness."

TSH:mbk
3/80

Walter Nugent

INDIANA UNIVERSITY DEPARTMENT OF HISTORY
Ballantine Hall
Bloomington, Indiana 47405
(812) 337-

FALL 1 9 8 1

History H655, Colloquium in Recent American History
Social and Political History 1865-1920

Text: none required
Class meetings: Thursdays 4pm - 6pm (except weeks 2 + 7: meet Tuesday)
PLACE - NOTE CHANGE: LI 651, not 851

Exams and papers: none (probably)
Reading assignments: weekly, ad hoc

Bibliography: some books are on Reserve. Others are in stacks, as are
Nugent's office hours: BH730, T2:30-3:30, R2:30-3,   journal articles.
                                  and by apptmt.

General plan:

1 Sep 3   Organizational - brief

Demographic segment:

2 Sep 8   Demog. I: overview and general trends. Nature of hist. demog.
3 Sep 17 Demog.II: immigrants, blacks, women.
4 Sep 24 Demog.III: cities, Western history.

Economic segment:

5 Oct 1   Econ. I: business cycles, sectoral changes. Agriculture.
6 Oct 8   Econ.II: workers, labor. Regulation of business.

Political segment:

7 Oct 13 Pol. I: party coalitions, electoral shifts
8 Oct 22 Pol. II: Reconstruction and the South
9 Oct 29 Pol. III: Gilded Age and Populism
10 Nov 5   Pol. IV: Progressive Era

Social-cultural segment:

11 Nov 12 Ideas and institutions. Role of intellectuals. Org. of knowledge
12 Nov 19 Historians and historiography from Parkman through the progressive
13 Dec 3   Class structure and social control. Marx, Tocqueville, and the
14 Dec.10 Overviews of the period. Its significance   middle class.
                           in US history. World comparisons?

14

Demographic segment:

Sep 8: Overview, genl trends. Historical demography.

The concerns of historical demography.
Recent work in that field.
Long-term American population patterns. Fro tier-rural, metropolitan, etc.
Fertility and mortality
Types of migrations: international, i ternal, inter/intra-regional.
Age structure.
Qq: why have rates of population change varied?
    what are the consequences of those changes?
    how does demographic change relate to other social change over time?

Sep 17: Immigrants, blacks, women.

The pattern of immigration to the US: numbers, sources, destinations
Reasons for emigrating and immigrating. The push-pull model.
Back-migration
Immigration restriction and nativism

Blacks: when and why were they migrants.
Thomas' black-immigrant substitution effect
Ghettoes: the same or different for blacks and immigrants?

Women and recent work in women's history

Sep 24: Cities and the west.

American urbanization: unique?
Functions of cities: an economic typology and spatial distribution
City government
Urban demography. Fertility, migration.
Westward movements: who, where, why. Persistence of frontier into 20th c.
Did the frontier experience create, or shape, American character?

Bibliography:

New book that deals with many of these areas, but especially presents
periodization of American history based on population growth changes:

Nugent, Structures of American Social History. (IUP 1981). Reserve.

Bibliog. relating especially to Demog. I (overviews, etc):

    General treatments of various kinds:
Bowen, Ian. Economics and Demography. London 1976.
Cassedy, James H. Demography in Early America: Beginnings of the
    Statistical Mind 1600-1800. Cambridge 1969.
Davis, Kingsley. "The World Demographic Transition." The Annals, Jan 45.
Drake, Michael. Historical Demography: Problems and Projects. 1974,
    The Open University.
Easterlin, Richard A. "Factors in the Decline of Farm Family Fertility
    in the United States." J. Amer. Hist. Dec 76.
Easterlin. "Population Change and Farm Settlement in the Northern United
    States," J Econ Hist. March 76.
Forster, Colin, and G. S. L. Tucker. Economic Opportunity and White
    American Fertility Ratios 1800-1860. New Haven 1972.

Glass, D. V., and D.E.C. Eversley. Population in History. London 1965.
Gordon, Michael. The American Family in Social-Historical Perspective.
   New York 1971
Hareven, Tamara K. Anonymous Americans. Englewood Cliffs 1973.
Hareven, T.K., and Maris Vinovskis. Family and Population in Nineteenth-
   Century America. Princeton 1978.
Guillaume, P., and J.-P. Poussou. Démographie Historique. Paris 1970.
Hollingsworth, T. H . Historical Demography. London 1969.
Lee, Ronald D. Population Patterns in the Past. New York 1977. [esp.
   McInnis' essay on fertility in 19th c. Ontario]
Matras, Judah. Introduction to Population. Englewood Cliffs 1977.
Potter, J. "The Growth of Population in America 1700-1860." In Glass
   and Eversley, pp 631-88.
Rabb, Theodore, and Rotberg, Robert. The Family in History. New York 1971.
Reinhard, Marcel, André Armengaud, and Jacques Dupâquier. Histoire générale
   de la population mondiale. Paris 1968.
Sauvy, Alred. General Theory of Population. NY 1969 [Paris about 1961]
Seward, Rudy Ray. The American Family: a Demographic History. Berverly
   Hills 1978.
Sharlin, Allan N. "Historical Demography as History and Geography." The
   American Behavioral Scientist, Nov-Dec 1977.
Thernstrom, Stephan, and Richard Sennett. Nineteenth Century Cities.
   New Haven 1969.
Vinovskis, Maris." The 1789 Life Table of Edward Wigglesworth." J EconH 9-71.
Wells, Robert V. The Population of the British Colonies in North America
   before 1776: a survey of census data. Princeton 1975.
Willcox, Walter, and Imre Ferenczi. International Migrations. 2v. NY:
   1929 and 1931.
Mitchell, B. R. European Historical Statistics. New York 1976.
US Census Bureau. Historical Statistics of the U.S....to 1970. Washington 75
Woytinsky, Wladimir. Die Welt in Zahlen. Berlin, 1920s.
   The best of Annales History:

Braudel, Fernand. The Mediterranean and the Med. World in the Age of
   Philip II. NY 1972, or 3d French edition, Paris 76.
Goubert, Pierre. Beauvais et le Beauvaisis de 1600 à 1730. Paris 1960.
LeRoy Ladurie, E. Les paysans de Languedoc.

   Fertility:

Grabill, Wilson H., et al., "A Long View". in Michael Gordon [above]
Hareven, T., and Maris Vinovskis. On fertility in two wards of Boston,
   late 19th c. J. Social History spring 75.
Leet, Don R. Review of Vinovskis' Demographic history and the world
   population crisis. J. Interdisciplinary Hist. aut. 78.
Lindert, Peter H. Fertility and Scarcity in America. Princeton 78.
Smith, Daniel Scott, and M. S. Hindus. "Premarital pregnancy in America
   1640-1971. J. Interdisc. Hist., spring 75.

   Mortality:

Condran, Gretchen A., and Eileen Crimmins. "A description and evaluation
   of mortality data in the federal census 1850-1900. Hist. Methods win 79
Fogel, Robert W., et al. "The economics of mortality in North Amerca
   1650-1910: a description of a research project. Hist. Methods spring 78.
Higgs, Robert. "Mortality in rural America 1870-1920." Explorations in
   Economic History, winter   73.
Higgs, R. "Cycles and Trends of Mortality in Eighteen Large American
   Cities 1871-1900." Expl. Econ. Hist. Oct 79.

Meeker, Edward. "The improving health of the United States 1850-1915." Expl. Econ. Hist. summer 72.

Rural:

Barron, Hal Seth. "The impact of rural delopulation on the local economy: Chelsea, Vermont 1840-1900." Agric. Hist. April 1980.

Bateman, Fred, and James D. Foust. "A sample of rural households selected from the 1860 manuscript census." Agric. Hist. Jan 74.

Danhof, Clarence. Change in Agriculture: the Northern United States 1820-1860. Cambridge 1969.

Shover, John L. First Majority-Last Minority: the transforming of rural life in America. DeKalb, 1976.

Stillwell, Lewis. "Migration from Vermont 1776-1860." Proceedings of the Vermont Historical Society 1937.

Other more-or-less general: (age, vertical mobility and stratification)

Achenbaum, W. A. Old Age in the New Land. 1978

Ingham, John N. "Rags to riches revisited: the effect of city size and related factors on the recruitment of business leaders." JAH Dec 76.

Modell, John, et al. "The timing of marriage in the transition to adulthood." In John Demos and Sarane S. Boocock, eds., Turning Points: Historical and Sociological Essays on the Family. Chicago 1978. [Also appeared in American J. Sociology, v. 84, 1978]

Parker, William N. "From Northwest to Mid-West: social bases of a regional history." In David Klingaman and Richard Vedder, Essays in Nineteenth Century Economic History: the Old Northwest. Athens 1975.

Pope, Clayne T., and Larry T. Wimmer. "Notes on the Genealogical Society Library and Its Data Sources." Paper at Chicago conference 1980.

Smith, Daniel Scott. "A community-based sample of the older population from the 1880 and 1900 U.S. Manuscript Census." Hist. Methods spring 78.

Stommel, Henry, and Elizabeth Stommel. "The year without a summer." Scientific America June 79.

Thompson, Warren S., and P. K. Whelpton. Population Trends in hhe United States. NY 1933.

Jensen, Richard. "History from a Deck of IBM cards." Reviews in American History, June 78.

Fischer, David H. Growing Old in America. New York 1977.

Kett, Joseph F. Rites of Passage: Adolescence in America. 1977.

Walker, Mack. Germany and the Emigration. Cambridge 1964.

Pessen, Edward. Riches, Class, and Power before the Civil War. Boston 73.

Soltow, Lee. Men and Wealth in the United States 1850-1870. New Haven 75.

Bibliography relating especially to Demog. II:

Immigration: (and migration generally)

Barr, Alwyn. "Occupational and geographic mobility in San Antonio." Social Science Quarterly, Sept 70.

Bieder, Robert E. "Kinship as a factor in migration." J. Marriage and the Family, Aug. 73.

Knights, Peter R. The Plain People of Boston. NY 1971.

Thomas, Brinley. Migration and Economic Growth. 2d ed. Cambridge 1973.

Thernstrom, S., and P. Knights. "Men in Motion." J. Interd. Hist. 1970.

Gallaway, Lowell E., and Richard K. Vedder. "Mobility of Native Americans." J. Econ. Hist. June 71.

Runblom, Harald, and Hans Norman. From Sweden to America: a history of
    the migration. Minneapolis and Uppsala 1976.
Taylor, Philip. The Distant Magnet: European Emigration to the United
    States. NY 1971.

Barton, Josef. Peasants and Strangers. Cambridge 1975.
Bodnar, John,   Immigration and Industrialization: ethnicity in an
    American mill town 1870-1940. Pittsburgh 1977.
Bodnar. "Migration, kinship, and urban adjustment: Blacks and Poles in
    Pittsburgh 1900-1930." J. Amer. Hist. Dec 79.
Bodnar. "Immigration, Kinship, and the Rise of Working-Class Realism in
    Industrial America." J Social History fall 80.
Köllmann, Wolfgang, and Peter Marschalck. "German Emigration to the
    United States." Perspectives in Amer. Hist. 1973, 499-556.
Wakatsuki, Yasu. "Japanese Emigration to the United States." Perspectives
    in Amer. Hist. 1979, 387-516.
Caroli, Betty Boyd. Italian Repatriation. NY 1975.
Conzen, Kathleen N. Immigrant Milwaukee. Hambridge 1976.
Conzen. "Commentary: immigrants, immigrant neighborhoods, and ethnic
    identity." J. Amer. Hist. Dec. 79.
Erickson, Charlotte. British Immigrants in Industrial America. 1958.
Gibson, Cambell. "The contribution of immigration to the United States
    population growth 1790-1970." Int'l Migration Review, summer 75.
Golab, Caroline. Immigrant Destinations. Philadelphia 1977.
Goren, Arthur A. New York Jews ant the Quest for Community. NY 1970.
Handlin, Oscar. Boston's Immigrants. 1941
Handlin. The Uprooted. 1957
Hawgood, John. The Tragedy of German America. 1940.
Higgs, Robert. "Race, Skills, and Earnings 1909." J. Econ. Hist. July 71.
Higham, J hn. Strangers in the Land. 1954
Kessner, Thomas. The Golden Door: Italian and Jewish Immigrant Mobility
    in New York City 1880-1915. NY 1977.
Luebke, Frederick C. Immigrants and Politics: the Germans of Nebraska
    1880-1900. Nebraska 1969.
Juhnke, James C. A People of Two Kingdoms: the political acculturation
    of the Kansas Menn-nites. 1975.
Howe, Irbing. World of our Fathers. NY 1976.
Moltmann, Gunter. Deutsche Amerikaauswanderung im 19. Hahrhundert.
    Stuttgart 1978.
Nelli, Humbert. Italians in Chicago 1880-1930. NY 1970.
Perspectives in Amercan History, 1973: several long pieces on emigration.
Pleck, Elizabeth H. "A mother's wages: income-earning among married Italian
    and black women 1896-1911." Paper, SSHA meeting, 1978.
Rischin, Moses. The Promised City: New York's Jews 1870-1914. 1962.
Rolle, Andrew F. The Immigrant Upraised. Norman 1968.
Vecoli, Rudolph. "Contadini in Chicago." J Amer. Hist. Dec 64.
Ward, David. Cities and Immigrants. NY 1971.

H655 syllabus 1981 p 6

[Demog. II, cont.]

Afro-Americans:

Henri, Florette. Black Migration: the Movement North 1900-1920.
NY 1973.
Blassingame, John. [on blacks in Savannah 1865-80] J. Social Hist. sum 73
Pleck, Elkzabeth H. "The two-parent household: Black family structure in
late 19th century Boston." J Social History, fall 72.
Lammermeier, Paul J. "The urban Black family of the 19th century: a
study of Black family structure in the Ohio Valley 1850-1880."
J. Marriage and the Family, Aug. 73.
Gutman, Herbert G. The Black Family in Slavery and Freedom 1750-1925.
NY 1976.
Cohen, William. "Negro involuntary servitude after 1865." J. Southern
Hist., Feb. 76.
Eblen, Jack. "New estimates of the vital rates of the U.S. black popula-
tion during the 19th century." Demography, May 74.
Farley, Reynolds. Growth of the Black Population. Chicago 1970.
Furstenberg, Frank, et al. "The origins of the female-headed black
family." J. Interdisc. Hist., autumn 75.
Harris, William. On black families in Atlanta. J. Social Hist. spring 76.
Higgs, Robert. "The boll weevil, the cotton economy, and black migration
1910-1930." Agric. Hist., Apr 76.
Higgs, R. Competition and Coercion: Blacks in he American Economy
1865-1914.. Cambridge 1977.
Meeker, Edward, and James Kau. "Racial Discrimination and Occupational
Attainment at the turn of the century." Explor. in Econ. Hist. July 77.
Osofsky, Gilbert. Harlem: the making of a ghetto. 1966.
Porter, Kenneth W. "Negro labor in the western cattle industry."
Labor History, summer 69.
Scheiner, Seth. Negro Mecca [NY 1865-1920]. 1965
Spear, Allan. Black Chicago [1890-1920]. 1967.
Wiener, Jonathan. "Class structure and economic development in the American
South 1865-1955." Comments by Higgs and Harold D. Woodman. A.H.R. Oct 7!
Kusner, Kenneth. A Ghetto Takes Shape: Black Cleveland 1870-1930. 1979.

Women:

Banner, Lois. Women in Modern America: a brief history. NY 1974.
Brownlee, W.E., and Brownlee, M.H. Women in the American Economy: a
documentary history 1675-1929. New Yaven 1976.
Cott, Nancy, and Elizabeth Pleck, eds. A Heritage of her own: toward a new
social history of American women. NY 79.
Degler, Carl. At Odds. NY 1980.
Carroll, Berenice. Liberating Women's History. 1976.
Hartman, Mary, and Lois Banner. Clio's Consciousness Raised. 1974 [papers
from the 1st Berkshire Conference]
Flexner, Eleanor. Century of Struggle. 1959.
Hargreaves, Mary W. M. "Women in agricultural settlement of the Great
Plains." Agric. History, Jan 76.
Jeffrey, Julie Roy. Frontier Women. 1979
Rothman, Sheila. Woman's Proper Place: a history of changing thought and
practice 1870-present. 1980
Ryan, Mary P. Womanhood in America, from colonial times to the present. 75
Ryan. "Reproduction in American history." Review article of books by
Litoff, Mohr, and Reed. J. Interdisc. Hist. aut. 79.
Smith, Daniel S. "Family limitation, sexual control, and domestic feminism
in Victorian America." in Cott and Pleck, above.

19

Demography III: Cities and the West

Cities:

Barr, Alwyn. "Occupational and geographical mobility in San Antonio."
    Soc. Sci. Quarterly, Sept. 1970.
Barrows, Robert G. "A demographic analysis of Indianapolis 1870-1920."
    IU Ph.D. diss., 1977.
Chudacoff, Howard. "A new look at ethnic neighborhoods..." J. Amer.
    Hist., June 1973.
Holli, Melvin. Reform in Detroit: Hazen S. Pingree and Urban
    Politics. Oxford 1969
Mandelbaum. Seymour. Boss Tweed's New York. New York 1965.
McKelvey, Blake. The Urbanization of America, 1860-1915. Rutgers 1960.
Monkkonen, Eric H. The dangerous class. Crime and poverty in
    Columbus, Ohio, 1860-1885. Harvard 1975.
Reps, John. Cities of the American West: a history of frontier urban
    planning. Princeton 1999.
Thernstrom, Stephan, and Peter Knights. "Men in Motion." J. Interdisc.
    Hist. 1970.
Thernstrom, Stephan. Poverty and Progress: social mobility in a nine-
    teenth century city. Harvard 1964.
Thernstrom, Steph, and Richard Sennett. Nineteenth Century Cities. 1969.
Sennett, Richard. Families against the city: middle class homes of
    industrial Chicago, 1872-1890. Harvard 1970.
Ward, David. Cities and Immigrants. 1971.
Warner, Sam B. Streetcar Suburbs: the process of growth in Boston
    1870-1900. Harvard 1962.
Weber, Adna Ferrin. The Growth of Cities in the Nineteenth Century:
    a Study in Statistics. New York, 1899.

West:

Billington, Ray Allen. Westward Expansion. 4th ed. New York 1982
Billington, Ray Allen. "Frederick Jackson Turner and the Closing
    of the Frontier." In Roger Daniels, ed., Essays in Western
    History in Honor of T. A. Larson. Laramie, 1971.
Burns, Venola L. "The diary of Luna Warner, a Kansas teenager of
    the early 1870s." Kansas Hist. Quart., autumn 1969, winter 1969.

(West, continued).

Bowden, Martyn J. "The Great American Desert and the American frontier, 1800-1882: popular images of the Plains." In Tamara Hareven, ed., Anonymous Americans. Englewood Cliffs, 1971.

Danhof, Clarence H. Change in Agriculture: the Northern United States, 1820-1870. Harvard 1969.

Denevan, William M., ed. The Native population of the Americas in 1492. Madison, 1976.

Driver, Harold E. Indians of North America. 2d ed. Chicago 1969.

Dykstra, Robert. The Cattle Towns. 1968.

Easterlin, Richard £. "Population change and farm settlement in the northern United States." Comments by Allan Bogue. J. Econ. Hist., March 1976.

Fite, Gilbert C. The Farmers' Frontier. New York 1966.

Gates, Paul W. "The Homestead Act in an Incongruous Land System." Amer. Hist. Rev., July 1936.

Glaab, Charles N. Kansas City and the Railroads: Community Policy in the Growth of a Regional Metropolis. Madison, 1962.

Gressley, Gene. Bankers and Cattlemen. New York, 1966.

Hollon, W. Eugene. Frontier Violence: Another Look. New York 1974.

Johnson, Anna D. "Rough was the road they journeyed." Palimpsest May-June 1977.

Larsen, Lawrence H. The Urban West and the End of the Frontier. Lawrence, Kan., 1978.

Martin, Calvin. Keepers of the Game: Indian-Animal Relationships and the Fur Trade. Berkeley 1978.

Paul, Rodman W. Mining Frontiers of the Far West. NY 1963.

Ramirez, Nora. "The Vacuero." IU Ph.D. diss., 1978.

Socolofsky, Homer. "Land disposal in Nebraska, 1854-1906: the Homestead story." Nebraska History, autumn 1967.

Socolofsky, Homer. "Success and failure in Nebraska homesteading." Agricultural History, April 1968.

Turner, Frederick Jackson. "The significance of the frontier in American history." Proceedings of the A.H.A., 1893, or in Turner, ed., The Frontier in American History (New York, 1 20).

Ubelaker, Douglas H. "Prehistoric New World population size: historical review and current appraisal..." Amer. J. Physical Anthropology, November 1976.

White, Richard. "The winning of the West: the expansion of the western Sioux in the 18th and 19th centuries." J. Amer. Hist. Sept. 78

Wishart, David. "Age and sex composition of the population on the Nebraska frontier." Nebraska History, spring 1973.

Borah, Woodrow. "Renaissance Europe and the Population of America." Revista de Historia [São Paulo] 1976.

Jacobs, Wilbur R. "The Tip of an Iceberg: Pre-Columbian Indian Demography and some Implications for Revisionism." Wm. and Mary Q., Jan. 1974.

INDIANA UNIVERSITY

DEPARTMENT OF HISTORY
Ballantine Hall
Bloomington, Indiana 47405
(812) 337-

H655 syllabus (continued)   Fall 1981

Economic segment

5. October 1. Economics I:
    Business cycles, sectoral shifts. Their determinants.
    The public sector.

    How to describe, then explain, the bsiness sycle from the
       Civil War to World War I? Why swings between depfessions
       and prosperity?
    The frontier-rural mode: agricultural expansion and productivity.
    The contours of change in manufacturing and transportation.
    What was the role of human capital? women, blacks, immigrants?
    Government and the economy: was it the heyday of laissez faire?

6. October 8. Economics II:
    Farmers and industrial workers. Government regulation. Big business.
    Socialiaation of workers. The question of worker control.
    The shifting nature of the middle class.
    Anti-trust legislation and kts background.

Bibliography:

for Economics I:
Aldrich, Mark. "A note on railroad rates and the Populist uprising."
    Agricultural History, July 1980.
Chandler, Alfred D. Strategy and Structure. 1962
Chandler, A. D. "The beginnings of big business in American industry."
    Business History Review 1959.
Evans, George H. Business incorporations in the United States 1800-1943.
    1948.
Farnham, Wallace D. "The weakened spring of government." Amer.
    Hist. Review 1963.
Fine, Sikdney. Laissez Faire and the General Welfare State. 1956
Fite, Gilbert C. "Southern agriculture since the Civkl War: an
    overview."" Agric. Hist., Jan 1979.
Galambos, Louis. The public image of big business in America
    1880-1940. 1975
Guither, Harold D. Heritage of Plenty: a guide to the economic
    history and development of U.S. agriculture. 1972
Higgs, Robert. "Railroad rates and the Populist uprising." Agric.
    Hist., July 1970.
Higgs, Robert. Transformation of the American Economy 1865-1914.
    1970.
Hoffmann, Charles. The Depresion of the Nineties. 1970
Keller, Morton. The Life Insurance Enterprise. 1963
Keller, Morton. Affairs of State: public life in late 19th century
    America. 1976
Long, Clarence D. Wages and earnings. . . 1860-1890. 1960

Output, Employment, and Productivity in the U.S. after 1800. 1966
Rees, Albert. Real Wages. . . 1890-1914.
Robertson, Ross. lHistory of American Economic Growth.
Salsbury, Stephen. "Economic history then and now: "The Economic
    History of the United States" in light of recent scholarship."
    Agric. History Oct 1979.
Vatter, Harold. The Drive to Industrial Maturity 1860-1914. 1975
Friedman, Milton, and Anna J. Schwartz. A Monetary History of the
    United States. 1968
Brownlee, W. Elliott. The Dynamics of Ascent. 1979.

for Econ. II:
Benson, Lee. Merchants, Farmers and Railroads. 1955
Cassity, Michael. (article on modernization and Knights of Labor).
    Journal of Amer. Hist. 1979
Grob, Gerald. Workers and Utopia (Knights of Labor) 1961
Gutman, Herbert G. "Work, Culture and Society in industrializing
America 1815-1919." Amer. Hist. Review 1973.
Kolko, Gabriel. Railroads and Regulation.
Lebergott, Stanley. The American Economy.   1976
Martin, Albro. Enterprise Denied.
Miller, George H. Railroads and the Granger Laws. 1971.
Purcell, Edward. "Ideas and Interests." J. Amer. Hist. 1867
Ransom and Sutch. One Kind of Freedom: The Economic Consequences of
    Emancipation. 1979
Spahr, Charles. The Wealth of the American People.   1896
Taylor, George R., and Irene Neu. The American Railway Network. 1956
Wall, Joseph F. Andrew Carnegie. 1970
Ware, Norman F. The Labor Movement in the U.S. 1860-1890. 1956
Weinstein, James. The Corporate Ideal in the Liberal State. 1960
Woodman, Harold D. "Chicago Businessmen and the Granger Laws."
    Agric. Hist. Apr 1962
Woodman, Harold D. "Sequel to Slavery." review article, J. Southern
    History, 1977, 523ff.
Yearley, Clifton K. The Money Machines. 1970

INDIANA UNIVERSITY | DEPARTMENT OF HISTORY
Ballantine Hall
Bloomington, Indiana 47405
(812) 337-

H655 syllabus, continued. Political segment

7. Politics I: parties, elections
    Democrats and Republicans: Tweedledum and Tweedledee?
    Party coalitions and electoral balances. Critical elections, if any
    Assigning activism or negativism to the parties. An era of laissez faire
        in politics?
    The narrative of elections and isues 1872-1889
    The federal response to emerging isues: rapid or slow?
    Party coalitions: sectional, cultural, economic

8. Politics II: Reconstruction and the postbellum South

    The Reconstruction narrative: several phases
    Role of the Radical Republicans:
    Why did the Radicals disappear?
    Constitutional aspects of Reconstruction
ec What happened to the former slaves?
    Carpetbaggers, scalawags, terrorists: who were they?
    Redeemers and Bourbons: persistent Whiggery?
    Disfranchisement and the rise of Jim Crow

9. Politics III: The late 19th century and Populism
    Elections and issues, 1870s and 1880s (continued from Politics I)
    Evaluating ethnocultural and economic explanations of the politics of
        the period: Kleppner-Jensen vs. Beard-Josephson
    Why the upheaval of 1890-96? Was there truly a "crisis of the 90s"?
    The nature, sources, and other aspects of Populism.

10. Politics IV: Politics of the Progressive Era
    Distinguishing New Freedom and New Nationalism
    Was progressivism a middle class movement? If so who were the m.c.?
    Why was there no socialism in the United States?
    Was progressivism motivated by class or status? or neither?
    The diversity of progressives and progressive measures
    Was progressivism continuous with Populism, or not?

I   October 13 [N.B. TUESDAY]
II   October 22
III October 29
IV   November 5

24

Bibliography relevant especially to Politics I:

Barnes, James.   Jolh G. Carlisle
Barr, Alwyn.   From Reconstruction to Reform [Texas]
Benson, Lee.   Merchants, Farmers, and Railroads
Blodgett, Geoffrey.   "The Mugwump Reputation 1870opresent".   J. Amer. Hist. 3-80
Carpenter, John A.   Ulysses S. Grant
Degler, Carl.   "American political parties and the rise of the city."   J. Amer.
    Hist. 6-64.   [or, reprinted in Jerme Clubb and Howard Allen, Electoral Change
    and Stability]
DeSantis, Vibuent.   The Republicans face the Southern Question.
Garraty, John.   The New Commonwealth [the 1880s]
Gould, Lewis L.   Wyoming, a political history
Hair, William Ivy.   Bourbonism and agrarian protest [Louisiana]
Hammarberg, Marvyn.   The Indiana Voter
Hirshson, Stanley.   Farewell to the Bloody Shirt
Hoogenboom, Ari.   Outlawing the Spoils
Josephson, Matthew.   The Politicos
Keller, Morton.   Affairs of State
Marcus, Robert.   Grant Old Party
Miller, George H.   Railroads and the Granger Laws
Nugent, Walter,   "Politics from 1877 to 1900."   In Wm. Cartwright and Richard
    Watson, The Reinterpretation of American History and Culture
Nugent, Walter.   Money and American Society 1865-1880
Rothman, David.   Politics and Power [the Senate]
Sharkey, Robert.   Money, Classand Party
Sproat, John G.   The Best Men [Mugwumps, et al]
Unger, Irwin.   The Greenback Era
Welch, Richard.   George Frisbie Hoar and the Half=Breed Republitans
Nevins, Allan.   Grover Cleveland.

Politics II:

Benedict, Michael Les.   Impeachment and Trial of Andrew Johnson
Brodie, Fawn.   Thaddeus Stevensz
Coben, Stanley.   "Northeastern Business and Radical Reco nstruction."   Miss.
    Valey Historical Review 6-59
Cox, John, and Cox, LaWanda.   Politics, Princiiple, and Prejudice
Donald, David.   Charles Sumner and the Rights of Man
DuBois, William E. B.   Black Reconsturction
Everson, Judith L.   "The Abolitionist Remnant" IU PhD diss.
Franklin, John Hope.   Reconstruction after the Civil War.
Franklin, John Hope.   "Mirror for Americans: a century of Reconstruction .his-
    toriography."   Amer. Hist. Rev. 2-1980
Harris, William C.   The Day of the Carpetbagger: Republican Reconstruction
    in Misissippi
Higgs, Robert.   Competition and Coercion: Blacks in the American Economy 1865-1914
Hume, Richard L.   "Carpetbaggers in the Reconstruction South". J. Amer. Hist. 9--77
Hair, William I.   Bourbonism and Agrarian Protest
Kousser, J. Morgan.   The shaping of Southern politics: suffrage restrictions
    and the establishment of the one-party South 1880-1910
Litwack, Leon.   Been in the Storm So Long

H655 syllabus p 13

McKitrick, Eric. Andrew Johnson and Reconstruction
Nugent, Walter. The Money Question during Reconstruction
Randall, J. G., and David Donald. Civil War and Reconstruction [1969 ed.]
Rose, Willie Lee. Rehearsal for Reconstruction.
Sharkey, Robert. Money, Class, and Party
Stampp, Kenneth. The Era of Reconstruction
Trelease, Alan. White Terror
Weisberger, Bernard. "The dark and bloody ground of Reconstruction
    historiography." J. Southern Hist. 1959
Woodward, C. Vann. Origins oc the New South 1877-1913
Woodward. Reunion and Reaction. [also, Allan Peskin article in J. Amer.
    Hist. 6-73, and Woodward's reply]
Woodward. The Strange Career of Jim Crow

Politics III:

Cherny, Robert. Populism to Progressivism in Nebraska
Cherny. Rebuttal to Goodwyn, in Great Plains Quarterly, su-mmer 1981
Clanton, Gene. Kansas Populism: ideas and men
Goodwyn , Lawrence. Democratic Promise
Hawkney, Sheldon. Populism to Progressivism in Alabama]
Hicks, John D. The Populist Revolt
Jensen, Richard. Winning of the Midwest
Kleppner, Paul. The Cross of Culture
Kleppner. The Third Electoral System 1853-1892
McSeveney, Samuel. The Politics of Depresion
Nugent, Walter. The Tolerant Populists. Kansas Populism and Nativism
Nugent. "Some Parameters of Populism." :Agric. Hist. 10-66
Parsons, Stanley. The Populist Context.
Rogin, Michael. "Californai Populism and...1896." Western Polit. Q. 3-69
[Parsons paper on cooperatives - Nugent has copy]
Turner, James. "Understanding the Populists." J. Amer. Hist. 9-1980
Argersinger, Peter. Populism and Politics: William Alfred Peffer...
Durden, Robert F. The Climax of Populism; the election of 1896
Larson, Robert W. New Mexico Populism
Gould, Lewis L. Wyoming
Morgan, H. Wayne. From Hayes to McKinley
McMath, Robert. Popular Vanguard
Spence, Clark. Territorial politics and government in Montana
Coletta, Paolo. William Jennings Bryan
Morgan, H. Wayne. William McKinley and his Amerifca

Politics IV

Allswang, John. A House for all peoples. [Democratic party]
Blum, John M. The R epublican Roosevelt
Cooper, J. M. "Racism and reform: a review essay." Wis. Mag. of History
    spring 1972
Davis, Allen F. Spearheads for Reform
Davis. American Heroine [Jane Addams]
Degler, on political parties and rise of the city -- above
Gordon, Lynn. "Women and the anti-child labor mlvement in Illinois 1890-
    1920." Social Service Review. June 1977
26

Gould, Lewis L.. Progressives and prohibitionists: Texas Democrats in the
    Wilson era
Graham, Otis. Encore for Reform
Haber, Samuel. Efficiency and Uplift
Flexner, Eleanor. Century of Struggle
Hays, Samuel P. :The politics of reform in municipal government in the
    Progressive Era." Pacific Northwest Quarterly 10-64
Hechler, Kenneth. Insurgency
Huthmacher, J. Joseph. "Urban liberalism and the age of reform." Miss.
    Valley Hist. Rev. 9-62
Filler, Louis. Crusaders for American Lib3ralism
Karl, Barry. Executive reorganization and reform in the New Deal
Kennedy, David M. "Overview: theprogressive era." Historian 5-75
Kennedy. Over Here [home front in World War I]
Link, Arthur S. Woodrow Wilson and the Progressive era.
Link. Woodlrow Wilson [many-volumed biography]
Lubove, Roy. The progressives and the slums
Lubove. The professional altruist
Lynch, Frederick. "Social theory and the Progressive Era." Theory and Society -4
Mowry, George.   The era of Theodore Roosevelt
Steffens, Lincoln. Autobiography
Thelen, David. "Social Tensions and the origins of Progressivism." J. Amer.
    Hist. 9-69
Thelen. The New Citizenship
Trattner, Walter. Crusade for the Children
Wendt, Lloyhd, and Herman Kogan. Lords of the Levee [reprinted as Bosses of
    Lusty Chicago]
Wiebe, Robert. Businesmen and reform
t. Troen, Selwyn. "The discovery of adolescence 1880-1920." in Lawrence
    Stone, Schooling and Society
Croly, Herbert. The Promise of American Life.
Steel, Ronald. Walter Lippmann

Social-cultural segment:

12 Nov 19 Ideas and institutions. Darwinism. Formalism. Reform.
13 Dec 3 Historians and historiography: Parkman to the progressives
14 Dec 10 Overviews of the period. The question of American exceptionalism.

Nov. 19: Ideas and institutions, etc.
        Was there such a thing as "formalism" (as Morton White said),
            and was there a revolt against it?
        What effects did Darwin and Spencer have on science, theology,
            and social thought?
        How and why did higher learning and the learned and practical
            professions develop in this period?
        What ideas of community, and of social thought otherwise,
            flourished during the progressive era? Was reform a
            disguise for social control by elites?

Bledstein, Burton. The Culture of Professionalism
Carter, Paul. Spiritual Crisis of the Gilded Age.
Cremin, Lawrence D. Transformation of the School.
Davis, Allan. American Heroine [Jane Addams]
Furner, Mary O. Advocacy and Objectivity
Gilbert, James. Designing the Industrial State: the intellectual pursuit
                of collectivism...
Haller, John S. Outcasts from Evolution
Hofstadter, Richard. Social Darwinism in American Thought
Kelley, Robert. The Transatlantic Persuasion
Lubove, Roy. The Professional Altruist
May, Henry F. Protestant Churches and Industrial America
May, Henry F. The End of American Innocence
Noble, David. The Paradox of Progressive Thought
Steffens, Lincoln. Autobiography
Veysey, Laurence. The Emergence of the American University
White, Morton. Social Thought in America: the revolt against formalism
Wilson, R. Jackson. In Quest of Community
James, William. Pragmatism
Hollinger, David A. "The problem of pragmatism in American history."
    Journal of Amer. Hist. 67, June 1980, 88-107.

Dec. 3   Historians and historiography

Relativism vs. Ranke
The frontier vs. the germ theory
What was or is progressive history?
Narration and literature
The main ideas of Turner, Beard, Becker

Adams, Henry. Any of the nine volumes of Jefferson-Madison
Beard, Charles A. An Economic Interpretation of the Constitution.
Beard. "That Noble Dream." In AHR 1935, or Fritz Stern, Varieties of Hist.
Becker, Carl. "Everyman his own historian."   1935 book of that name.
Benson, Lee. Turner and Beard
Billington, Ray A. Frederick Jackson Turner
Billington. "The OAH in the bad old days." JAH 6-78, 75-84.
Higham, John. History. Chaps. 1-3
Hofstadter, Richard. The Progressive Historians
Henretta, James. "Social History as lived and written." AHR 12-79
    with comments by Berkhofer and Rutman
Kammen, Michael. Introductory chapter in Kammen, ed., The Past Before us.
Mink, Louis O. "History and fiction as modes of comprehension."
    New Literary History [Charlottesville, Va.], spring 1970.
Parkman, Francis. Any volume of France and England
Strout, Cushing. The Pragmatic Revolt in American History: Carl Becker
    and Charles Beard.
Turner, Frederick Jackson. "The Significance of the Frontier in American
    History." Loss of places, but esp. The Frontier in American History,1920
Wish, Harvey. The American Historian. [chaps. 6-14]

Dec. 10 Overviews of the period

What theme, device, or principle(s) best synthesizes the 1865-1920
period? How can we pull it together? Where does it fit in American
history or general history?

Bender, Thomas. Community and Social Change in America.
Buenker, John D. "The Progressive Era." Mid-America July 1969.
Hays, Samuel P. The Response to Industrialism.
Morgan, H. Wayne. The Gilded Age. [2d ed.]
Nugent, Walter. From Centennial to World War.
Rodgers, Daniel. The Work Ethic in Industrial America.
Veysey, Laurence. "The Autonomy of American History Reconsidered."
    American Quarterly 31, fall 1979, 455-79.
Walker, Robert H. The Gilded Age

Also, appropriate chapters in Cartwright and Watson, and Kammen (The
    Past Before Us)

29

HISTORY C18-1
Mr. Roeder
Fall, 1979

The US Since the 1890s: Encountering
Limits to Growth, 1890-1920

Instructor: George H. Roeder, Jr.
Office: 12-D, Harris Hall
Phone: 492-7261
Home Phone: 864-3351
Office Hours: 1:00-2:50 Wednesday, 11:00-11:50 Friday, and
               by appointment

Required Reading:

Samuel P. Hays, The Response to Industrialism, 1885-1914 (By Oct. 3)
Upton Sinclair, The Jungle (Oct. 15)
David P. Thelen, Robert M. La Follette and the Insurgent Spirit (Oct. 26)
James J. Flink, The Car Culture (Nov. 9)
John M. Cooper, Jr., ed., Causes and Consequences of World War I (By
    Nov. 26)

Books on reserve:

Alfred D. Chandler, The Visible Hand: The Managerial Revolution in
                    American Business
Melvyn Dubofsky, We Shall Be All: A History of the Industrial Workers
                 of the World
Herbert G. Gutman, Work, Culture & Society in Industrializing America
Aileen S. Kraditor, The Ideas of the Woman Suffrage Movement, 1890-1920
N. Gordon Levin, Jr., Woodrow Wilson and World Politics: America's
                      Response to War and Revolution
Arthur S. Link and William B. Catton, American Epoch: A History of the
                                       United States Since 1900: VOLUME
                                       ONE, 1900-1920
Henry F. May, End of American Innocence: A Study of the First Years of
              Our Own Time, 1912-1917
William L. O'Neill, Divorce in the Progressive Era
William Preston, Jr., Aliens and Dissenters: Federal Suppression of
                      Radicals, 1903-1933
Robert H. Wiebe, The Search for Order, 1877-1920

Grading:

Mid-term exam, Wednesday, October 31 (25% of course grade)

Research paper due Friday, November 30 (40%)

Final exam,

Both of the exams will include short-answer and essay questions.

See separate sheet giving instructions for research paper.

HISTORY C18-1   Fall, 1979

INSTRUCTIONS FOR RESEARCH PAPER

1. Write a research paper on a topic which contributes to your
understanding of ideas, events, trends, movements, or people discussed in this course. The paper should be approximately 8 to 12
typewritten pages in length and must relate clearly to themes
developed in course readings and lectures.

2. Although you may consult books and articles written by historians
in writing this paper, you should rely mainly on the types of raw
materials which historians themselves use in composing their works --
oral history interviews and sources from the period under study
such as newspapers, magazines, government documents, trade journals,
works of fiction, manuscript collections, and artifacts. I do not
want you to base your paper on polished sources which have organized
the material for you. I want you to take on the challenge of con-
structing a coherent story or analysis from the scattered, sometimes
confusing, sometimes contradictory verbal and material records which
serve as our link to the past.

3. By the end of the quarter I want you to know more about the topic
than anyone else in the class, including me. I want to learn something
from your paper which I will be able to use to improve one of my
lectures. Pick your topic with this in mind. Do not write on a
broad topic such as "The United States in World War I." Pick a more
precisely focused topic such as "Women Workers in the Automobile
Industry During World War I." A well focused topic does not have
to be a narrowly conceived topic. Do not shy away from the big
questions if they are appropriate to your topic. Use your specialized
knowledge to throw light on larger issues.

4. Feel free to discuss your paper with other students, but the
organization and wording of the paper must be your own. Mention in
footnotes at appropriate points any source which you draw on heavily
or which you quote or paraphrase. Use common sense in preparing
your footnotes. They serve their purpose if they enable the reader
to locate easily the source of particular quotation, paraphrase, or
concept.

5. Save all of the notes which you make while doing research for the
paper. If you wish to discuss your paper as you are writing it or
after it has been graded, I may ask you to bring your notes to the
discussion. Often the strengths and weaknesses of a paper can be
understood more clearly by both teacher and student through a review
of the student's approach to taking research notes.

6. Write a paper which does not deserve any of the following comments:
"you rely too heavily on one or two sources in which the author has
already organized the material for you"; "you do nothing to place your
topic in a historical context, or to show how it relates to themes
developed in this course"; "poor writing and organization obscure the
points which you are trying to make"; "you do little more than restate
the obvious - your paper lacks the fresh insights which result from
imaginative research and from taking the time to subject your ideas
to thorough analysis"; "you should reread every sentence in this paper
and ask yourself after reading each one, 'do I really believe that?'"

7. My natural inclination to give students the highest grade I
can without undermining this institution's demanding standards
of academic excellence will grow weaker every day after Friday,
November 30, when the paper is due.

Undergraduate

PRINCETON UNIVERSITY

HISTORY 382

Fall Term 1983-84   Prof. Challener and Weiss

The United States: The 1890s to 1941

Format: Two lectures, Monday and Wednesday at 10:00 a.m. Films as noted
below on Monday nights at 7:30 p.m.

Recommended Purchases

    Robert Beisner, From the Old Diplomacy to the New
    Samuel P. Hays, The Response to Industrialism, 1885-1914
    Walter LaFeber, The New Empire
    Emily S. Rosenberg, Spreading the American Dream: American Economic
       and Cultural Expansion, 1890-1945
    William Appleman Williams, The Tragedy of American Diplomacy
    Jane Addams, Twenty Years at Hull-House
    John M. Blum, The Republican Roosevelt
    Moses Rischin, The Promised City: New York's Jews, 1870-1914
    Gilbert Osofsky, Harlem: The Making of a Ghetto
    David M. Kennedy, Over Here: The First World War and American Society
    Robert and Helen Lynd, Middletown
    Joan Hoff Wilson, Herbert Hoover: Forgotten Progressive
    William E. Leuchtenburg, Franklin D. Roosevelt and the New Deal
    Alan Brinkley, Voices of Protest: Huey Long, Father Coughlin, and the
       Great Depression
    Robert A. Divine, The Reluctant Belligerent: American Entry into
       World War II

Material on Reserve at Firestone Library

    Richard Hofstadter, "Manifest Destiny and the Philippines,"
       in Daniel Aaron, ed., America in Crisis
    Frederic C. Howe, Confessions of a Reformer
    Robert H. Wiebe, The Search for Order
    Walter LaFeber, The Panama Canal
    James C. Thomson, Jr., Peter W. Stanley, and John Curtis Perry,
       Sentimental Imperialists: The American Experience in East Asia
    Leonard Dinnerstein, "A Dreyfus Affair in Georgia," in Dinnerstein, ed.,
       Antisemitism in the United States
    Nancy J. Weiss, "The Atlanta Race Riot of 1906 and the Ordeal of
       Segregated Black America" (mimeographed)
    Arthur S. Link, Woodrow Wilson and the Progressive Era
    Arthur S. Link, Wilson the Diplomatist
    Arthur S. Link, "What Happened to the Progressive Movement in the 1920s?"
       (Bobbs-Merrill reprint)
    Robert Dallek, The American Style of Foreign Policy
    Barton J. Bernstein, "The New Deal: The Conservative Achievements of
       Liberal Reform" (Bobbs-Merrill reprint)
    Ronald Radosh, Prophets on the Right

In addition, a few copies of each of the books listed under "Recommended
Purchases" have been placed on reserve in order to accommodate those
students who choose not to buy the books.

33

Schedule of Lectures, Films, and Reading Assignments

Week of September 12

    Lectures: (1) Introductory Themes
               (2) From Isolationism to Imperialism

    Readings: Robert Beisner, From the Old Diplomacy to the New, pp. 3-106
              Samuel P. Hays, The Response to Industrialism, 1885-1914
                  pp. 1-162, 188-93

Precepts will not meet this week.

Week of September 19

    Lectures: (1) The New Manifest Destiny and the Splendid Little War
               (2) Progressivism and the Flowering of Political and
                    Social Change: I

    Readings: Walter LaFeber, The New Empire, pp. 150-96, 284-417
              Richard Hofstadter, "Manifest Destiny and the Philippines,"
                  in Daniel Aaron, ed., America in Crisis, pp. 173-200
                  (Reserve)
              Emily S. Rosenberg, Spreading the American Dream: American
                  Economic and Cultural Expansion, 1890-1945, pp. 1-62
              William Appleman Williams, The Tragedy of American
                  Diplomacy, pp. 3-57

Week of September 26

    Lectures: (1) Progressivism and the Flowering of Political and
                   Social Change: II
              (2) The Far East from McKinley to Wilson

    Readings: Frederic C. Howe, Confessions of a Reformer,
                  pp. 1-8, 40-131 (Reserve)
              Jane Addams, Twenty Years at Hull-House, pp. 60-132,
                  148-68, 200-238 (chps. 4-8, 10, 13-14)
              Robert H. Wiebe, The Search for Order, pp. xiii-xiv,
                  111-13, 127-32, 164-89 (Reserve)

Week of October 3

    Lectures: (1) The Caribbean as an American Lake
               (2) Seeking Access to the System: Immigrants and the
                    Process of Acculturation

    Readings: John M. Blum, The Republican Roosevelt
              Walter LaFeber, The Panama Canal, pp. 3-57, 217-27 (Reserve)
              James C. Thomson, Jr., Peter W. Stanley, and John Curtis
                  Perry, Sentimental Imperialists: The American Experience
                  in East Asia, pp. 44-92, 106-53 (Reserve)

Week of October 10

Lectures: (1) Seeking Access to the System: The Struggle for
                Racial Equality
           (2) Seeking Access to the System: The Campaign for
                Women's Rights

Readings: Moses Rischin, The Promised City, pp. 51-111, 144-48, 171-267
           Gilbert Osofsky, Harlem: The Making of a Getto, pp. 17-67,
                71-91, 105-23, 127-87
           Leonard Dinnerstein, "A Dreyfus Affair in Georgia," in
                Dinnerstein, ed., Antisemitism in the United States,
                pp. 87-101 (Reserve)
           Nancy J. Weiss, "The Atlanta Race Riot of 1906 and the
                Ordeal of Segregated Black America" (Reserve)

Film: "Hester Street" 10 McCosh, 7:30 p.m.

Week of October 17

Lectures: (1) The Road to War and Plans for a New World Order
           (2) Woodrow Wilson and the League of Nations

Readings: Arthur S. Link, Woodrow Wilson and the Progressive Era,
                pp. 1-24, 34-60, 223-51 (Reserve)
           Arthur S. Link, Wilson the Diplomatist, pp. 3-125 (Reserve)
           David M. Kennedy, Over Here: The First World War and American
                Society, pp. 45-143, 231-95

Film: "Woodrow Wilson" 101 McCormick, 7:30 p.m.

Week of October 24   MID-TERM RECESS

Week of October 31

Lectures: (1) Versailles and Its Aftermath
           (2) Adapting to the Postwar World

Readings: Arthur S. Link, "What Happend to the Progressive Movement
                in the 1920s?" (Reserve)
           Robert Dallek, The American Style of Foreign Policy,
                pp. 92-122 (Reserve)

MID-TERM EXERCISE: Pick up 9:00 a.m., Monday, October 31, History Office,
                      129 Dickinson Hall; due there no later than 4:00 p.m.,
                      Monday, November 7.

Week of November 7

Lectures: (1) Understanding the 1920s
           (2) The Republican Era in Foreign Policy: From Normalcy
                to Depression

Readings: Robert and Helen Lynd, Middletown, pp. 3-178, 225-312, 413-502

Film: "Inherit the Wind" 101 McCormick, 7:30 p.m.

35

Week of November 14

Lectures: (1) Exit Prosperity, Enter Depression
            (2) Focus on the White House: FDR as Presidential Hero

Readings: Joan Hoff Wilson, Herbert Hoover: Forgotten Progressive,
              pp. 79-208
            Emily S. Rosenberg, Spreading the American Dream:
              American Economic and Cultural Expansion, 1890-1945,
              pp. 108-60

Film: "Gabriel over the White House" 10 McCosh, 7:30 p.m.

Week of November 21

Lectures: (1) Foreign Policy and the National Mood in the 1930s
            (2) From Progressivism to the New Deal

Readings: William E. Leuchtenburg, Franklin D. Roosevelt and the
              New Deal, pp. 41-196, 231-348

Film: "Franklin D. Roosevelt" 101 McCormick, 7:30 p.m.

Week of November 28

Lectures: (1) The New Deal and American Society
            (2) The United States and the Coming of the War

Readings: Alan Brinkley, Voices of Protest: Huey Long, Father
              Coughlin, and the Great Depression, pp. 3-168, 192-215
            Barton J. Bernstein, "The New Deal: The Conservative
              Achievements of Liberal Reform" (Reserve)

Film: "The Grapes of Wrath" 101 McCormick, 7:30 p.m.

Week of December 5

Lectures: (1) How Far Had We Come? The Legacy of the New Deal
            (2) How Far Had We Come? The End of Isolationism

Readings: Robert A. Divine, The Reluctant Belligerent: American
              Entry into World War II
            Ronald Radosh, Prophets on the Right, pp. 11-65, 119-46,
              (Reserve)
            William Appleman Williams, The Tragedy of American
              Diplomacy, pp. 162-201

Film: "War Comes to America" 101 McCormick, 7:30 p.m.

BROWN UNIVERSITY

Mr. Patterson

American History 1880s to 1930

This course will explore various aspects of American history, except for foreign affairs, from the 1880s to 1930. Required readings listed below will be available, in paper, at the bookstore. Also on 3-hour reserve at the library (one copy only).

John Buenker, et al, Progressivism
Norman Clark, Deliver Us From Evil
John Dos Passos, The Big Money
Melvyn Dubofsky, We Shall Be All
Lawrence Goodwyn, The Populist Moment
William Harbaugh, Life and Times of Theodore Roosevelt
Samuel Hays, Response to Industrialism
John Kasson, Amusing the Millions
David Kennedy, Over Here
Aileen Kraditor, Ideas of the Womens Suffrage Movement
Robert & Helen Lynd, Middletown
James Weinstein, Corporate Ideal in the Liberal State

There will also be required articles--on 3-hour reserve at the library. Look for under title of journal or book.

Students with little background in American history may wish to read a textbook. Copies of mine, entitled America in the 20th Century: A History, are available in paper at the bookstore.

Discussions will ordinarily replace one of the three lectures per week. Occasionally, there will be three lectures plus a discussion. Discussion leaders are Mr. Gillon and Ms. Jirgensons.

These discussions are central to the course. You should attend all of them and be prepared to discuss the week's readings. Attendance and performance in sections may affect your grade. Section leaders will ordinarily grade papers and exams.

Written Assignments and Exams:

1. Required midterm, written in class, Oct. 19.

2. Required final exam, Saturday, Dec. 17, 2 p.m. Potential questions to be distributed a week or so in advance.

3. Book review (c. 4 pp), evaluating one assigned book (except Lynd or Dos Passos). Due at start of appropriate section discussion.

4. Review essay, comparing two or three books (10-15 pp) that deal with some important question in U.S. History, 1880-1930. Due Dec. 5.

For example of different types of review essays, see essays in New York Review of Books; or (most useful) Reviews in American History; or "model" essays on reserve. These "models" will be xerox copies of "Work and the Working Class"; "Feminist Thought, 1963-70"; and

"Italian Immigrant Adjustment to American Society" in Twentieth
Century History Journal (phony title), done by Able Student(s); and
shorter reviews by Banner, Harper, & O'Neill, in Reviews in American
History, June 1975 and stapled together. Ask for journal titles at
Reserve desk.

All papers must be polished, proofread, and properly footnoted. We
will judge papers for style and organization as well as for originality of ideas and depth of research.

See your section instructor and/or Mr. Patterson no later than mid-
term, in order to settle on manageable topics. If you wait longer,
you may well have a serious problem finding books.

Students who write review essays may wish to focus on subjects
covered in part by readings and lectures. To encourage such essays,
we list below some possible topics, with books you might read.
Note that regularly assigned books are at the top of some of these
lists. If you include such assigned books in your reviews (which
we recommend as a way of developing a depth of knowledge, and of
critical understanding), you should also include TWO additional
books from that list. (Do not choose the book you review in your
other 4-page review.) If you do not use a regularly assigned book,
select two non-assigned books to form the basis of your essay.
Feel free also to include other relevant books or articles, pro-
viding that you do not exceed the recommended length of 10-15 pages.

Books starred (*) will be available in paper at the bookstore. All
will be on 3-hour reserve at the library.

Students who elect to write essays on different subjects from those
suggested here, or who use books not listed below, may do so, with
the permission of section instructor.

Suggested Topics for Comparative Essays:

1. Race and the City

   Kenneth Kusmer, A Ghetto Takes Shape (Cleveland)*
   Gilbert Osofsky, Harlem: Making of a Ghetto*
   William Tuttle, Race Riot (Chicago, 1919)*

2. Populism

   Lawrence Goodwyn, Populist Moment*
   John Hicks, Populist Revolt*
   Norman Pollack, Populist Response to Industrial America*

3. Labor

   Melvyn Dubofsky, We Shall Be All*
   Herbert Gutman, Work, Culture, and Society in Industial America*
   David Brody, Steelworkers in America*
   Nick Salvatore, Eugene Debs

4. Women

Aileen Kraditor, Ideas of the Womens Suffrage Movement*
Allen Davis, American Heroine (Jane Addams)*
Sheila Rothman, Womens Proper Place*
Mari Jo Buhle, Women and American Socialism*

5. Politics

William Harbaugh, Life and Times of TR*
John Blum, Woodrow Wilson and the Politics of Morality*
David Thelen, Robert La Follette and the Insurgent Spirit*
David Burner, Politics of Provincialism (Dems. 1918-32)*

6. Prohibition and Social Change

Norman Clark, Deliver Us From Evil*
James Timberlake, Prohibition and the Progressive Movement*
Joseph Gusfield, Symbolic Crusade*

Grading:

The final exam will count for approximately 40% of your grade, the
papers 40%, the midterm 20%. Note the "approximately". Attendance
and performance at sections are very important and may affect grading.

Assignments:

Week of:
Sept. 5   Begin Hays. No discussion.

Sept. 12   Hays 1-162, 188-93. Discussion #1.

Sept. 19   Dubofsky, v-xi, 5-172, 227-285, 471-84. Discussion #2.

Sept. 26   Goodwyn, Intro., parts 1, 3. Also James Turner "Under-
             standing the Populists," Journal of American History,
             67 (Sept. 1980), 354-73. Discussion #3.

Oct. 3   Kasson. Also John Higham, "Reorientation of American
             Culture in the 1890s," in Higham, Writing American
             History, 73-117. Discussion #4.

Oct. 10   Buenker. Also Daniel Rogers, "In Search of Progressiv-
             ism," in Stanley Kutler and Stanley Katz, eds., The
             Promise of American History, 113-132. Discussion #5.

Oct. 17   Harbaugh, chapts. 7-10, 13-15, 18-21, 23-27, 30-31.
             No discussion.

Oct. 19   MIDTERM (covering assignments through week of Oct. 10).

Oct.   24   Weinstein, 1-171. Also William Graebner, "Federalism in the Progressive Era: A Structural Interpretation of Reform," Journal of American History, 64 (Sept. 1977), 331-57. Discussion #6.

Oct.   31   Kraditor, pp. v-xvi, 1-13, 43-74, 123-173, 197-264. Discussion #7.

Nov.   7   Clark, 1-13, 68-180, 209-26. Discussion #8.

Nov.   14   Kennedy, 3-191, 231-295; Weinstein, 214-54. Discussion #9.

Nov.   21   Begin Lynds. No Discussion.

Nov.   28   Lynds, chapts. 1-12, 24-29. Discussion #10.

Dec.   5   Dos Passos. No Discussion.

Dec.   5   Papers due. No extensions granted.

Reading Period. Complete Dos Passos.

Final Exam: Saturday, Dec. 17, 2 p.m. Attendance required. No excuses.

PRINCETON UNIVERSITY
Department of History

HISTORY 590

THE UNITED STATES SINCE 1920

Term: Spring 1983
GRADUATE COURSE

Professor Richard D. Challener
Professor Nancy J. Weiss

History 590, the last part of the four-term graduate reading course
cycle in American history, is designed to introduce the student to some
of the most important aspects of the history of the United States since
1920. Assigned readings focus on major political, diplomatic, economic,
and social issues. The approach is topical within a chronological
framework.

Class discussions each week will be based primarily on the general
assignment. We have deliberately limited the number of books students
are expected to read in order to allow for close analysis of each of
the works. In addition to the general assignment, each student will
be expected to prepare three or four short review essays on the books
listed below. The review essays will be discussed in class. Students
should deposit a copy of each essay in the History Graduate Study Room
and give one copy to each instructor no later than the Monday morning
preceding the Wednesday when the essay will be discussed. Specific
instructions for the preparation of the essays will be given at the
introductory seminar meeting.

The Assigned readings and books for review have been selected with
an eye to raising major issues of interpretation and method while at the
same time introducing students to some of the newest and most provocative
literature in the field. These readings are by no means exhaustive, and
students who are already familiar with them will doubtless want to read
more widely. Anyone preparing a field in modern American history will
certainly need to do so. For that purpose, we have prepared a separate
list of suggestions for additional reading, which will be distributed
at the first class meeting.

It will be assumed that participants in the seminar have a basic
textbook knowledge of the history of the period covered by History 590.
Anyone for whom this is not the case should consult a good textbook --
for example, Arthur S. Link and William B. Catton, American Epoch: A
History of the United States since 1900 (5th ed.), William F. Leuchtenburg,
ed., The Unfinished Century: America since 1900, or James T. Patterson,
America in the Twentieth Century (2nd ed.).

February 9   POLITICS OF THE REPUBLICAN ERA

Assigned

David Burner, Herbert Hoover: A Public Life
Allan J. Lichtmen, Prejudice and the Old Politics: The Presidential
    Election of 1928

Review Essays

1. Joan Hoff Wilson, Herbert Hoover:, Forgotten Progressive
2. Albert U. Romasco, The Poverty of Abundance: Hoover, The Nation,
   the Depression, and Murray Rothbard, "The Hoover Myth," Studies
   on the Left, VI (July-August 1966), 70-84.

February 16   THE NEW DEAL

Assigned

James MacGregor Burns, Roosevelt: The Lion and the Fox
Frank Freidel, Franklin D. Roosevelt: Launching the New Deal

Review Essays

1. Arthur M. Schlesinger, Jr., The Coming of the New Deal
2. Ellis W. Hawley, The New Deal and the Problem of Monopoly

February 23   POLITICS OF THE RIGHT AND LEFT

Assigned

Alan Brinkley, Voices of Protest: Huey Long, Father Coughlin, and the
    Great Depression
Paul K. Conkin, The New Deal
Barton J. Bernstein, "The New Deal: The Conservative Achievements of
    Liberal Reform," in Bernstein, ed., Towards a New Past, pp. 263-88

Review Essays

1. T. Harry Williams, Huey Long
2. Arthur M. Schlesinger, Jr., The Politics of Upheaval

March 2   THE NEW DEAL AND FOREIGN POLICY

Assigned

Warren Cohen, The American Revisionists: The Lessons of Intervention
    in World War I
Ronald Radosh, Prophets on the Right: Profiles of Conservative Critics
    of American Globalism, pp. 11-65, 119-46
Either Henry Feingold, The Politics of Rescue: The Roosevelt Administration
    and the Holocaust, 1938-1945, or Walter Laqueur, The Terrible Secret:
    Suppression of the Truth about Hitler's 'Final Solution'

Review Essays

1. Robert Dallek, <u>Franklin D. Roosevelt and American Foreign Policy,
   1932-1945</u>
2. William L. Langer and S. Everett Gleason, <u>Challenge to Isolation,
   1937-1940</u>

March 9   WORLD WAR II AND THE ORIGINS OF THE COLD WAR

Assigned

John Lewis Gaddis, <u>The United States and the Origins of the Cold War</u>
John Lewis Gaddis, <u>Strategies of Containment: A Critical Appraisal
    of Postwar American National Security Policy</u>, pp. 1-126
Michael Sherry, <u>Preparing for the Next War: American Plans for
    Postwar Defense, 1941-1945</u>

Review Essays

1. Gabriel Kolko, <u>The Politics of War: The World and U. S. Foreign
   Policy, 1943-1945</u>
2. Daniel Yergin, <u>Shattered Peace: The Origins of the Cold War and
   the National Security State</u>

March 23   POLITICS OF THE 1940s

Assigned

John Morton Blum, <u>V Was for Victory: Politics and Culture during
    World War II</u>
Alonzo L. Hamby, <u>Beyond the New Deal: Harry S. Truman and American
    Liberalism</u>, pp. xiii-xx, 3-85, 121-351, 505-16
Robert H. Ferrell, <u>Harry S. Truman and the Modern American Presidency</u>

Review Essays

1. Robert J. Donovan, <u>Conflict and Crisis: The Presidency of Harry
   S. Truman, 1945-1948</u>, and <u>Tumultuous Years: The Presidency of
   Harry S. Truman, 1949-1953</u>
2. James T. Patterson, <u>Mr. Republican: A Biography of Robert A. Taft</u>

March 30   McCARTHYISM

Assigned

Michael Paul Rogin, <u>The Intellectuals and McCarthy</u>
Richard Hofstadter, "The Pseudo-Conservative Revolt - 1954," in
    <u>The Paranoid Style in American Politics</u>, pp. 41-65
Seymour Martin Lipset and Earl Raab, <u>The Politics of Unreason:
    Right-Wing Extremism in America, 1790-1970</u>, pp. 209-47
Nelson W. Polsby, "Towards an Explanation of McCarthyism," <u>Political
    Studies</u>, VIII (Oct. 1960), 250-71
Talcott Parsons, "Social Strains in America," in Daniel Bell, ed.,
    <u>The New American Right</u>, pp. 117-40
C. Vann Woodward,"The Populist Heritage and the Intellectual,"
    <u>American Scholar</u>, XXIX (Winter 1959-60), 55-72

Review Essays

1. Thomas C. Reeves, The Life and Times of Joe McCarthy
2. Robert Griffith, The Politics of Fear: Joseph R. McCarthy
    and the Senate

April 6   THE EISENHOWER ERA

Assigned

Fred Greenstein, The Hidden-Hand Presidency: Eisenhower as Leader
Robert Griffith, "Dwight D. Eisenhower and the Corporate Commonwealth,"
    American Historical Review, LXXXVII (Feb. 1982), 87-122
John Lewis Gaddis, Strategies of Containment, pp. 127-97

Review Essays

1. Herbert S. Parmet, Eisenhower and the American Crusades
2. Townsend Hoopes, The Devil and John Foster Dulles

April 13   CIVIL RIGHTS

Assigned

August Meir, "On the Role of Martin Luther King," New Politics,
    IV (Winter 1965), 52-59
William H. Chafe, Civilities and Civil Rights: Greensboro, North Carolina,
    and the Black Struggle for Freedom
Clayborne Carson, In Struggle: SNCC and the Black Awakening of the 1960s

Review Essays

1. Stephen B. Oates, Let the Trumpet Sound: The Life of Martin Luther
    King, Jr.
2. David J. Garrow, Protest at Selma: Martin Luther King, Jr., and
    the Voting Rights Act of 1965

April 20   THE WOMEN'S MOVEMENT

Assigned

William H. Chafe, The American Woman: Her Changing Social, Economic,
    and Political Roles, 1920-1970
Sheila M. Rothman, Woman's Proper Palce: A History of Changing Ideals
    and Practices, 1870 to the Present, chs. 4-7
Sara Evans, Personal Politics: The Roots of Woman's Liberation in
    the Civil Rights Movement and the New Left

Review Essays

1. Winifred Wandersee, Women's Work and Family Values: 1920-1940
2. Susan Ware, Beyond Suffrage: Women in the New Deal

April 27   THE NEW FRONTIER AND THE GREAT SOCIETY

Assigned

Samuel H. Beer, "In Search of a New Public Philosophy," in Anthony King,
    ed., The American Political System, pp. 5-44
James T. Patterson, America's Struggle against Poverty, 1900-1980
Henry J. Aaron, Politics and the Professors: The Great Socity in Perspective

Review Essays

1. Sar A. Levitan and Robert Taggart, The Promise of Greatness, and
    Marvin E. Gettleman and David Mermelstein, eds., The Great
    Society Reader: The Failure of Americal Liberalism
2. Theodore J. Lowi, The End of Liberalism

May 4   NEW PERSPECTIVES ON THE PRESIDENCY

Assigned

Garry Wills, The Kennedy Imprisonment
Robert A. Caro, The Years of Lyndon Johnson: The Path to Power,
    introduction and chs. 5, 7, 8, 11, 13, 15, 16, 19, 21, 23, 26,
    28-37
Fawn M. Brodie, Richard Nixon: The Shaping of His Character

No Review Essays

1/26/83 (cs) 35

Mr. Patterson   History 170   Spring 1981

This course will focus on American history from 1930 to c. 1970. No systematic coverage of foreign policy. Readings below are available in paperback, and on 3-hour reserve at the library. They are:

Stephen Ambrose, Rise to Globalism
John Blum, V Was for Victory (World War II)
Richard Cloward & Frances Fox Piven, Regulating the Poor
Vivian Gornick, Romance of American Communism
Robert Griffith, Politics of Fear   (McCarthyism)
Doris Kearns, Lyndon Johnson & the American Dream
Alonzo Hamby, Beyond the New Deal   (Truman years)
William Leuchtenburg, Franklin D. Roosevelt & the New Deal
Anthony Lewis, Gideon's Trumpet   (Supreme Court)
David Lewis, King
Jonathan Schell, Time of Illusion
Warren Susman, ed., Culture & Commitment, 1929-1945
Richard Wright, American Hunger
Richard Wright, Uncle Tom's Children

Students with limited background, or who feel the need for a supplementary narrative, may wish to read volume 2 of my text, America in the Twentieth Century. Available in paper at the bookstore.

Articles on Reserve:

Richard Rovere, "Eisenhower Revisited..." NY Times Mag., 2/7/71

Articles at Bookstore:

Jerold Auerbach, "New Deal, Old Deal, or Raw Deal..." Journal of
   Southern History, 1969, 18-30 (Bobbs-Merrill Reprint H-359)
Carl Degler, "Ordeal of Herbert Hoover," Yale Review, 1963, pp. 563-83.
   (Bobbs-Merrill Reprint H-52).

Written Assignments:

Students will have the following option. Either:

a. Research paper (c. 10-15 pp). Use primary sources.

b. Essay (c. 10-15 pp), on some important aspect of recent U.S. history. Based on two or three outside books. See below for suggested topics based in part on regularly assigned readings.

For samples of such essays, see articles in Reviews in American History, in periodicals reading room, or New York Review of Books. See also "model" student essays on reserve. These are listed under the phony title of Twentieth Century History Journal. Titles include "Work and the Working Class," "Feminist Thought, 1963-70", and "Italian Immigrant Adjustment to American Society." Ask for these at reserve desk under journal title.

46

All papers due May 11, by 4 p.m., in History office in B-12,
Alumnae Hall. They should be polished, proof-read, and properly
footnoted. They will be judged for style and organization as well
as for originality of ideas and depth of research.

Those who choose to write the essays may wish to use regularly
assigned readings as a springboard into your topics. Such essays
would include one or two books from assigned readings and two outside books. Some possible topics are suggested here. All books
listed are available in paper (in limited quantities) at the bookstore.

1. Hoover, FDR, and the Depression

Leuchtenburg, FDR and the New Deal
Joan Hoff Wilson, Herbert Hoover
Ellis Hawley, New Deal and the Problem of Monopoly

2. Social Change in America, 1930-70

Lynd (s), Middletown in Transition
Blum, V Was for Victory
Richard Polenberg, One Nation Divisible (class and ethnicity)
William Leuchtenburg, Troubled Feast (social change)

3. The Underclasses   (do 2, plus Wright)

Wright, American Hunger/Uncle Tom's Children
Carol Stack, All Our Kin (black life in the city)
Elliot Liebow, Tally's Corner (black life in the city)
Joseph Howell, Hard Living on Clay Street (poor whites)

4. Policy-Making in the Postwar Era

Cloward and Piven, Regulating the Poor
Hamby, Beyond the New Deal
Daniel Moynihan, Maximum Feasible Misunderstanding (war on poverty)
Theodore Lowi, End of Liberalism

5. Postwar Critics of American Life (use all three)

Christopher Lasch, Culture of Narcissism
Charles Reich, Greening of America
Paul Goodman, Growing Up Absurd

Students opting for different subjects, or for the research paper,
must see instructor by midterm. Consult supplementary lists.

Examinations:

There will be a three-hour final exam, at the regularly scheduled time. Toward the end of semester, potential exam questions will be distributed.

The midterm, required, will be a 50-minute exam, in class, March 16. It will cover work done through March 13.

Grading:

Final exam will count for approximately 40%, the paper 40%, the midterm 20%. Note the "approximately." Attendance and performance in sections are very important, and will often affect grades.

Assignments:

Week of:

Jan. 26   Wright

Feb. 2   Finish Wright books

Feb. 9   Susman, 1-45, 60-92, 126-219, 236-61, 297-370.
           Discussion #1 (on Susman).

Feb. 16   Leuchtenburg, chs. 1-8; Degler.

Feb. 23   Leuchtenburg, chs. 10,11,14;
           Cloward and Piven, Intro., chapts 2-5.
           Auerbach article. <u>Discussion #2</u>.

March 2   Blum, entire. <u>Discussion #3</u>.
           Ambrose, chapts 1-3

March 9   Hamby, chs. 1-6, 8-15, 17, 20-23.
           Ambrose, chapts 4-7   <u>Discussion #4</u>. (on Hamby)

March 16   MIDTERM EXAM, in class hour

March 16   Griffith, chs. 1-4, 6-9, Concl.
           Rovere article
           Ambrose, chapts 8-9

March 23   Gornick, pp. 3-144, 190-241, 256-65.
              Discussion #5 (on Griffith and Gornick)

April 6   Lewis (Gideons Trumpet) Discussion #6.

April 13   Lewis (King), chs. 3, 5-9, 11-Epilogue. Disc. #7.

April 20   Kearns. Discussion #8 (on Kearns).
           Ambrose, chapts 10-12.

April 27   Schell.
           Finish Ambrose.

Reading Period. Finish Schell.

Final Exam

Princeton University

HISTORY 383

THE UNITED STATES SINCE 1940

Spring 1983
Undergraduate

Professor Challener
Professor Weiss

Format: Two lectures, Tuesday and Thursday at 11:00 a.m. in Mccosh 50.
One preceptorial to be arranged. Films as noted below on
Tuesdays at 7:30 p.m. in McCosh 10 (note, however, that the
film on March 8 is in Peyton).

Suggested Purchases

John Morton Blum, V Was for Victory: Politics and American Culture
During World War II
William H. Chafe, The American Woman: Her Changing Social, Economic
and Political Roles, 1920-1970
John Lewis Gaddis, The United States and the Origins of the Cold War,
1941-47
Thomas G. Patterson, On Every Front: The Making of the Cold War
John Lewis Gaddis, Strategies of Containment: A Critical Appraisal
of Postwar American National Security Policy
Harvard Sitkoff, The Struggle for Black Equality, 1954-1980
William H. Chafe, Civilities and Civil Rights: Greensboro, North
Carolina, and the Black Struggle for Freedom
Robert W. Griffith, The Politics of Fear: Joseph R. McCarthy and the
Senate
Godfrey Hodgson, America in Our Time
David Halberstam, The Best and the Brightest
Jonathan Schell, The Time of Illusion

Material on Reserve at Firestone Library

J. Joseph Huthmacher, Trial by War and Depression
Alonzo L. Hamby, "The Vital Center, the Fair Deal, and the Quest for a
Liberal Political Economy," American Historical Review, LXXVII (June
1972), 653-78
August Meier, "On the Role of Martin Luther King," New Politics, IV
(Winter 1965), 52-59
Robert Griffith, "Dwight D. Eisenhower and the Corporate Commonwealth,"
American Historical Review, LXXXVII (Feb. 1982), 87-122
Arthur M. Schlesinger, Jr., A Thousand Days: John F. Kennedy in the
White House
Richard J. Walton, Cold War and Counterrevolution: The Foreign Policy
of John F. Kennedy
Leslie H. Gelb, "Vietnam: The System Worked," Foreign Policy, III
(Summer 1971), 140-67
William Shawcross, Sideshow: Kissinger, Nixon and the Destruction of
Cambodia
Samuel H. Beer, "In Search of a New Public Philosophy," in Anthony
King, ed., The New American Political System, pp. 5-44
James T. Patterson, America's Struggle Against Poverty, 1900-1980
Henry J. Aaron, Politics and the Professors: The Great Society in
Perspective
Theodore H. White, America in Search of Itself

In addition, several copies of each of the books listed under "Suggested Purchases" have been placed on reserve to accommodate those students who choose not to buy the books.

Optional Textbook

There is no textbook assigned for this course. In the past, however, students who felt a lack of factual background have occasionally asked what they might read to tie the course together. Anyone who feels the need of a textbook should consult Arthur S. Link and William B. Catton, American Epoch, 5th ed., Vol. II: 1938-1980. Copies are available at the U-Store and at the Reserve Desk.

Schedule of Lectures, Films, and Preceptorial Assignments

Week of January 31

Lectures: (1) Introductory Meeting
            (2) 1941: The Domestic Agenda on the Eve of War

No precepts, but students who have not taken History 382 should familiarize themselves with Huthmacher, Trial by War and Depression, pp. 51-196 (Reserve).

No film.

Week of February 7

Lectures: (1) The Home Front: Domestic Perspectives on the Second World War
            (2) FDR as War Leader: Soldier of Freedom or Architect of Disaster?

Preceptorial Assignment: Blum, V Was for Victory, pp. 3-70, 90-167, 172-254
                          Chafe, The American Woman, pp. 135-95

Film: "Mission to Moscow"

Week of February 14

Lectures: (1) The UN and the Bomb: Two Strategies for Peace
            (2) The Shattered Peace: From the Yalta to the Riga Axioms

Preceptorial Assignment: Gaddis, The United States and the Origins of
                          the Cold War, pp. 1-243, 316-61

Films: "The Battle of San Pietro"
        "Hiroshima/Nagasaki, August 1945"

Week of February 21

Lectures: (1) Coming to Terms with the Truman Presidency
            (2) The Truman Revolution in Foreign Policy: Containment or Globalism?

Preceptorial Assignment: Patterson, On Every Front, pp. 1-173
                             Gaddis, Strategies of Containment, pp. 1-123
                             Hamby, "The Vital Center, the Fair Deal and the
                             Quest for a Liberal Political Economy" (Reserve)

Film: "Harry S. Truman"

Week of February 28

Lectures: (1)   Law as an Instrument of Social Change: Civil Rights in
                   Recent American Politics
          (2)   The China Tangle, Korea, and the Rise of the Nuclear
                   Deterrent

Preceptorial Assignment: Sitkoff, The Struggle for Black Equality, pp. 20-166
                             Chafe, Civilities and Civil Rights, Chaps. 2-5
                             Meier, "On the Role of Martin Luther King" (Reserve)

Film: "Raisin in the Sun"

Week of March 7

Lectures: (1)   Witch Hunt, Anticommunist Style: McCarthvism in American Life
          (2)   McCarthyism as Tragedy: Alger Hiss, Whittaker Chambers,
                   and John Foster Dulles

Preceptorial Assignment: Griffith, The Politics of Fear

Film: "See It Now"--Murrow-McCarthy broadcast, March 1954, and McCarthy's
answer, April 1954 (Peyton Hall)

Week of March 14   SPRING VACATION

Week of March 21

Lectures: (1)   Once Again, We Like Ike: Some Reflections on Dwight D.
                   Eisenhower
          (2)   The Eisenhower-Dulles Consensus in Foreign Policy: States-
                   manship or Brinkmanship?

Preceptiorial Assignment: Gaddis, Strategies of Containment, pp. 127-97
                          Griffith, "Dwight D. Eisenhower and the Corporate
                          Commonwealth" (Reserve)

No Film

MONDAY, MARCH 21:   PICK UP TAKE-HOME MID-TERM EXERCISE, 9:00 A.M., HISTORY
                       OFFICE, 129 DICKINSON HALL

MONDAY, MARCH 28:   TAKE-HOME EXERCISE MUST BE TURNED IN AT THE HISTORY OFFICE
                       NO LATER THAN 4:00 P.M.

Week of March 28

Lectures: (1) Separating John F. Kennedy from the Legend: What Are We
to Make of Camelot?
(2) A Knight Must be Invincible: Pigs, Walls, Missiles, and
Test Bans

Preceptorial Assignment: Schlesinger, A Thousand Days, pp. 194-278, 726-69,
811-43 (these pages refer to the paperback edition;
if you are using the hardback, you should read
pp. 206-97, 794-841, 889-923) (Reserve)
Walton, Cold War and Counterrevolution, pp. 3-10,
34-59, 103-61 (Reserve)

Film: "Dr. Strangelove"

Week of April 4

Lectures: (1) Falling Short of Presidential Greatness: The Paradox of
Lyndon B. Johnson
(2) Vietnam and the Fracturing of the Foreign Policy Consensus

Preceptorial Assignment: Halberstam, The Best and the Brightest, pp. 9-81,
247-368, 488-584, 714-809 (these pages refer to
the paperback edition; if you are using the hardback, you should read pp. 1-63, 200-301, 401-81,
588-665)
Gelb, "Vietnam: The System Worked" (Reserve)

Film: "Hearts and Minds"

Week of April 11

Lectures: (1) Struggles for Equality: Black Power, Women's Liberation,
and the Slow Transformation of American Society
(2) Coming Apart: The Legacy of the 1960s

Preceptorial Assignment: Hodgson, America in Our Time, pp. 3-18, 67-110,
134-84, 200-224, 244-364
Chafe, The American Woman, pp. 199-244

No film

Week of April 18

Lectures (1) The Nixon Administration, Watergate, and the Crisis of the
Imperial Presidency
(2) Nixon and Kissinger: Realpolitik, Game Plans, and Detente

Preceptorial Assignment: Schell, The Time of Illusion, pp. 5-74, 201-387
Shawcross, Sideshow, pp. 19-35, 112-86 (Reserve)
Gaddis, Strategies of Containment, pp. 345-57

Film: "All the President's Men"

Week of April 25

Lectures (1) Foreign Policy under Carter and Reagan: How Far Has the
              Pendulum Swung Back?
         (2) The 1970s: The End of Liberalism?

Preceptorial Assignment: Beer, "In Search of a New Public Philosophy"
                          (Reserve)
                          Patterson, America's Struggle Against Poverty,
                          pp. 78-114, 126-84 (Reserve)
                          Aaron, Politics and the Professors, pp. 1-10,
                          16-49, 146-67 (Reserve)
                          White, America in Search of Itself, pp. 99-164
                          (Reserve)

No film

Final Exercise

There will be a take-home final exercise during the examination period.
Dates and details will be announced later.

1/14/83 (dc)

HISTORY C18-3
Spring 1981

US HISTORY SINCE 1945

Instructor: George H. Roeder, Jr.
Office: 103-B Harris Hall
Phone: 492-7448 Home: 864-3351
Office hrs.: Wed. 11-12; Fri. 9-10
& by appointment

Required reading:

Stephen Ambrose, Rise to Globalism (complete by May 4)
Richard Polenberg, One Nation Divisible (May 4)
Studs Terkel, Working (May 15)
Eric Barnouw, Tube of Plenty (May 22)

Choose one of the following (complete by May 4):

Frances Fitzgerald, Fire in the Lake
David Halberstam, The Best and theBrightest
Guenter Lewy, America in Vietnam

Note that I have asked you to complete three books by May 4, the day of
the midterm exam. I recommend that you read through the Ambrose and
Polenberg as soon as possible, and then before each lecture reread the
material pertinent to that lecture. Note also that the final paper is
due near the time when you should complete the reading of Terkel and
Barnouw. Plan accordingly and do some of your reading in advance to give
yourself room to complete everything on time.

Grading:

Midterm exam, Monday, May 4, 30% of course grade
Report on Vietnam book, 30% of grade --
   rough draft due Friday, May 8, 10:00 a.m.
   final paper due Friday, May 18, 10:00 a.m.
   (penalty for late drafts and late papers)
There will be a final exam, Friday, June 5, 12:00-2:00

Schedule of classes:

March 30	Introduction
April 1	The Bomb
3	Power and Conflict: The Cold War
6	American Society in 1945
8	The Cold War and domestic affairs
10	Truman and Eisenhower: measuring differences
13	Korea: the other war
15	Affluence and anxiety
17	Kennedy and the election of 1960
20	LBJ and Nixon
22	Minorities, women, youth: common interests?
24	Security and subversion: Watergate and the C.I.A.
27	Jobs and the environment
29	Zero-sum society?
May 1	Discussion

May	4	Midterm exam
	6	Vietnam: Issues
	8	Vietnam: Impact
	11	Diversity, power, and conflict
	13	Work in America
	15	Institutionalized America
	18	The visual environment
	20	Truth in the marketplace
	22	The Tube of Plenty
	25	Memorial Day--no class
	27	The future in the past

Movies: (attendance recommended, but not required)

April 7 On the Beach

May 10 Another Family for Peace, and The War at Home

Instructions for paper: Write a six- to eight-page paper on one of the three books on Vietnam listed on the preceding page. In the paper do the following:

   summarize the book's main points and describe the arguments and evidence which the author uses in support of these points

   offer a critical analysis of the author's assumptions, arguments, and evidence -- in this analysis give examples of points which might be raised by readers who disagreed with the book's judgements and conclusions

   explain how a defender of the book might answer the objections raised in the critical analysis

   present, and defend, your own conclusions as to the validity of the main points made in the book -- if you conclude that you cannot make such judgments without further information, specify the information which you require

A note on grading: Although both exams will include short answer sections, roughly 75% of your grade will be based on the paper and on essay sections of the exam. Here are some guidelines which I keep in mind when grading essays or papers:

An "A" paper is one which is good enough to read aloud to the class. A typical "A" paper is clearly written, well organized, and offers perceptive general statements supported by a rich and well chosen variety of specific examples. Above all, it demonstrates that while taking the course the student has grappled with the issues raised in readings and lectures, and has developed the ability to write with intelligence and imagination on these issues.

A "B" paper is a solid piece of work which demonstrates that the student has a good understanding of material covered in the course. Many "B" papers would not be appropriate for reading aloud in class because they mainly provide a summary of ideas and information already presented in readings and lectures. Other "B" papers give evidence of independent thought on the student's part, but the ideas presented in these papers are not clearly and convincingly explained and defended.

A "C" paper provides a less thorough and accurate summary of material presented in the course, or a less adequate defense and explanation of the student's analysis of issues raised in the couse.

"D" and "F" papers do not respond adequately to the assigned questions, or are marred by the types of errors, unclear writing,and poor organization which indicate that the student does not understnd the material presented in the course.

INTRODUCTORY QUESTIONS

If you consider any of the following questions an unjustified invasion
of privacy, please do not answer the offending questions. Although I
do not want you to put your name on the questionnaire, sometimes the
identity of the student filling out a particular questionnaire is obvious

1. Give your age, sex, and your family's economic status (upper,
    upper-middle, etc.)

2. What interests, abilities, experiences, or expertise do you have
    which might allow you to make special contributions to a course
    on U.S. History since 1945?

3. What have been your main sources of information on American history?
    Courses? Discussion with family members or friends? Visits to
    historic sites and museums, or non-required reading?

4. How do you learn about current affairs? Which newspapers and
    magazines do you read, and with what regularity? What TV or radio
    news programs have served as important sources of information for
    you?

5. What events and developments of the past 35 years do you want to
    know more about?

iINTRODUCTORY QUESTIONS

6. Answer yes or no. Have you ever:

    Been east of the Appalachians?
    Been west of the Mississippi?
    Been west of the Rockies?
    Been outside of the United States?
    Crossed the Atlantic or Pacific?
    Been to Washington, D.C.?
    Been to the top of a building over 50 stories high?
    Flown in an airplane?
    Taken a trip on a train?
    Lived on a farm?
    Lived in a non-suburban town with population under 10,000?
    Worked in a factory?
    Worked for the government?
    Benn in the military?
    Voted?
    Participated in a riot or demonstration?
    Smoked pot?
    Been to an art museum?
    Been to an opera?
    Benn to a rock concert?
    Written a computer program?
    Become proficient with a musical instrument?
    Been to a professional football or baseball game?
    Eaten at McDonalds?
    Had strong religious faith?
    Witnessed the birth of a child?
    Been with someone at the moment of death?
    Cheated on a paper or exam?
    Been in jail?
    Met a Congressman, Senator, or other high government official?

7. What do you consider to be the most important differences between
    the experiences which you had during your first 20 years of life
    and the experiences which your parents had during their first 20
    years?

8. What ideas or facts have excited your imagination recently? What
    issues do you talk about with friends?

9. What are your favorite books and works of art. Who are your favorite
    authors and artists? Your favorite movies?

10. Briefly identify any of the following which are familiar to you:

Jackson Pollock

Ho Chi Minh

Teheran

Nagasaki

Pete Rose
Richard Schweiker

H. R. Haldeman

Al Pacino

Dean Rusk

Sam Peckinpah

Kent State

Jackson State

Philip Roth

Betty Friedan
Lee Harvey Oswald
NATO
Joe McCarthy
Willie Nelson

11. What pleases you most, and what displeases you most, about life in
     the United States in recent years?

QUEENS COLLEGE, CITY UNIVERSITY OF NEW YORK

Spring, 1982   HISTORY 69AA   PH 202
Michael Wreszin   The United States Since 1945   8:00 MW

This course is an increasingly selective survey of U.S. history from 1945 to the
present focusing on the following themes: American globalism from the Cold War
to Vietnam and beyond; the struggle for racial equality from civil rights to
black power to benign neglect and the revolt against affirmative action; the
prevailing political ideology from the Cold War consensus to New Left Conflict
to the Neo-Conservative Nationalists and the counter-culture movements from the
Beats, hippies and flower children to the sprited feminist movement of the present.

The following paperbound books have been ordered at the College Bookstore. They
are required reading.

Godfrey Hodgson, AMERICA IN OUR TIME, Vintage
Robert D. Marcus and David Burner, AMERICA SINCE 1945 (anthology)
Harvard Sitkoff, THE STRUGGLE FOR BLACK EQUALITY 1954 - 1980 Oxford
Saul Bellow, MR. SAMMLER'S PLANET, Penguin
Irwin Unger, THE MOVEMENT, Dodd Mead
Norman Podhoretz, BREAKING RANKS

There will be a midterm, a final and a writing assignment. What follows is a
tentative syllabus to help you order your reading.

1: Feb. 1   Introduction to Course. Discussion of course mechanics, reading
                 assignments, class participation, general outline of course and
                 introductory remarks on history as a discipline and the claims
                 of historical neutrality and detachment.

   Feb. 3   THE BOMB: TRUMAN AND THE ORIGINS OF THE COLD WAR
                 Film: The Bomb from series The World At War
                 Hodgson, chs. 1/3 pp. 3/47
                 Marcus and Burner (M&B) Bernstein, "The Cold War: Revisionist"
                 Harriman, Establishment pp. 3/48 LaFeber, Korean War 39/53

                 Question: Why were bombs dropped not one but two?

2: Feb. 8   Truman: COLD WAR ABROAD AND AT HOME

                 M&B, Army McCarthy Hearings 102/118, Kempton and Rovere conflicting
                 views of Eisenhower 84/101, Gary Wills on Nixon and "Checkers"
                 Speech 69/83, Podhoretz, BREAKING RANKS PROLOGUE AND BEGIN UP TO
                 119

3: Feb. 17 /   THE IKE AGE: THE IDEOLOGY OF LIBERAL CONSENSUS AND THE BEAT
   Mar. 1   CRITIQUE

                 Hodgson, chs. 4/7 65/152 (Pay VERY SPECIAL ATTENTION TO CH. 4,
                 THE IDEOLOGY OF LIBERAL CONSENSUS, PAGE 76 FF. Commit it to
                 memory if you have to and thoroughly try and understand its
                 political implications
                 M&B, Galbraith 119/129, Harrington 136/150

Question: What was Post-war liberalism attitude toward change,
welfare, toward womankind? Why was capitalism seen as revolutionary?
How would it solve Social Problems? What is meant by the "End of
Ideology?"

4: Mar. 3   The Beat Critique: Roots of the Counterculture of the 60s

Irwin Unger, The Movement, ch. 1 1/24
Hodgson 321/325   Students with a little iniative might want to
seek out Ginzberg's Howland, other works of the Beats in the library
Kerouac, Ferlinghetti. Norman Mailer's essay, The White Negro, is
in Advertisements for Myself.

5: Mar. 8 /   THE SECOND RECONSTRUCTION: CIVIL RIGHTS STRUGGLE 1945/1960
    Mar. 15
Read Hodgson, chs. 8 & 9, 153/199
Unger, Movement, chs. 2, 25/50
M&B, M.L. King, 130/135
Begin reading Sitkoff, Black Equality, pp. _____
Some questions: How was the Plessy vs. Ferguson decision
related to the idea of growth in the liberal ideology? Why
was the phrase "With all deliberate speed" such a cruel irony?
What ultimately was the principle tactic of integrationist civil
rights movements?

6: Mar. 17 /   THE NEW FRONTIER AND THE SECOND RECONSTRUCTION CONTINUED
    Mar. 22
Read: Podhoretz, chs. 7-10, pp. 188/170
M&B, Burner & West, "The Kennedy Nation," 168-182
JFK Inaugural Address, 183-187
Sitkoff, _____

*******************MIDTERM EXAM TENTATIVELY SCHEDULED FOR MARCH 24

7: Mar. 24/   WAR AND LIBERALISM: THE RESPONSIBILITY AND ARROGANCE OF POWER
    Mar. 29
Reread: M&B, "The Kennedy Nation"; Podhoretz, ch. 11, 170/194
Read: Hodgson, chs. 11/12, pp. 225-262
Begin reading: Sammler's Planet (read carefully and thoughtfully)
Was Kennedy's foreign policy different than Ike's? How so?

8: Mar. 31 / WAR AND LIBERALISM II: LBJ, GUNS AND BUTTER
    Apr. 14
Read: Hodgson, ch. 14, pp. 274/287
M&B, Michael Herr Dispatches, pp. 239/249
Keep reading Sammler
M&B, LBJ's Great Society Speech, pp. 224/227
Bellow, Sammler's Planet - almost finished?
Why were we fighting the war - what was the official explanation?
Was it clear to the Govt. leadership? Was it clear to the people
like Podhoretz? What was the relationship between the war and
watergate, if any? Possibly show the film Hearts and Minds one
afternoon this week.

62

9: Apr. 19 /   THE WAR AT HOME: THE CRISIS OF CULTURE
   Apr. 26
                 Read: Hodgson, chs. 15/17
Reading   Unger, The Movement, chs. 3,4, pp. 51/116
assignments   Podhoretz, Breaking Ranks, chs. 12/19, pp. 194/304
getting a bit   M&B, Port Huron Statement, 187/204
heavier.   Bellow, Sammler's Planet - class discussion on the 26th
It's good   What caused the crisis? What's the relationship between political
you got ahead   dissent and cultural rebellion? Are matters of "life style"
earlier   political issues? Have they always been? What are the implications
                 of a decline in fear/respect for authority? Does order, limits,
                 tradition, authority, insure justice?

10: Apr. 8 /   CRISIS OF CULTURE II: BLACK SEPARATISM - REVOLUTIONARY LIBERATION?
    May 3
                 Read: Hodgson, ch. 10, 200/224
                 Finish Sitkoff
                 M&B, Malcolm X on Revolution, pp. 220/223, Nixon, 306/316,
                 Unger, The Movement, chs. 5,6, 117/179
                 What was the real meaning of the revolutionary rhetoric of The
                 Black Panthers, The Weatherman of SDS? What really is the cause
                 of the decline of the movement for black liberation? Historically
                 speaking which movement served the black community as a whole
                 more effectively.

11: May 5 /   FROM BLACK REVOLUTION TO THE FEMINIST MOVEMENT
    May 12
                 Read: Hodgson, chs. 18-21, pp. 353/411
                 M&B, B. Friedan, "The Feminine Mystique," pp. 163/164
                 S. Evans, "Personal Politics," pp. 264/289
                 Unger, The Movement, ch. 7, pp. 180/208
                 Podhoretz - jump ahead and read his Postscript, pp. 361/367
                 Who and what institutions does the feminist movement allegedly
                 threaten? Is the movement still attracting younger women? Why
                 does it have a genuinely revolutionary potential - or does it?
                 Where did its recent revival come from?

12: May 17   THE GREAT REACTION: FROM NIXON TO CARTER TO REAGAN
                 Read: Hodgson, chs. 22-25, pp. 412/500
                 Podhoretz, pp. 304/358
                 M&B, Schell on Watergate, 281/298, Kissinger, pp. 316-32?
                 Thurlow, pp. 339/348, Wills on Reagan, pp. 349/354
                 Commoner, 298/305

UNIVERSITY OF VIRGINIA

Undergraduate course

HISTORY US 337

DIPLOMATIC HISTORY OF THE UNITED STATES TO 1920

Fall Semester 1983

Norman A. Graebner

Lecture Topics:

1. The European State System and the Imperial Conflict in America
2. The Diplomacy of Independence
3. Confederation and Constitution
4. Federalist Foundations
5. The Louisiana Purchase
6. The War of 1812 and the Treaty of Ghent
7. The Diplomacy of John Quincy Adams and the Monroe Doctrine
8. Jacksonians and Whigs
9. Manifest Destiny and the Texas Question
10. The Oregon Compromise
11. The Mexican War

Midterm

12. The Great Debate over the Monroe Doctrine, 1830-1860
13. Nonintervention and the Revolutions of 1848
14. The United States in the Far East, 1848-1860
15. Seward's Diplomacy, 1861-1862
16. Seward's Diplomacy, 1863-1866
17. The United States and Bismarck's Europe, 1870-1895
18. Interventionism and Latin America
19. Expansion into the Pacific, 1860-1900
20. The Broken Diplomatic Tradition
21. The Great Divide: The Summer of 1914
22. The Failure of American Neutrality
23. Crusade in Europe
24. Versailles and the Great Debate, 1919-1920

64

Books assigned to all students:

Thomas G. Paterson, et al, American Foreign Policy: A History to 1914
    (Heath, 1983).
Felix Gilbert, To The Farewell Address (Princeton, 1961).
Bradford Perkins, ed., The Causes of the War of 1812 (Krieger, 1976).
Frederick Merk, Manifest Destiny and Mission (Vintage, 1966).
H. Wayne Morgan, America's Road to Empire (Wiley, 1965).
Raymond A. Esthus, Theodore Roosevelt and the International Rivalries
    (Regina Books, 1982).
Ross Gregory, The Origins of American Intervention in the First World War
    (Norton, 1971).

Open Book examination due at the end of the fourth week:

This will be a 1200 to 1500-word essay, written in a blue book, on one of the
following questions based on Bradford Perkins's The Causes of the War of 1812:

Do maritime factors explain the War of 1812 better than internal factors?

What reasons did the West and South have for supporting a declaration of war
against Great Britain?

Assignment for the mid-term examination:

Paterson's American Foreign Policy, pp. 3-117.
The books by Gilbert and Merk.

Assignment for the final examination:

Paterson's American Foreign Policy, pp. 121-251.
The books by Morgan, Esthus, and Gregory.

UNIVERSITY OF VIRGINIA

Title: DIPLOMATIC HISTORY OF THE UNITED STATES SINCE 1920

Undergraduate course

HIUS 338

Spring Semester 1983   Norman A. Graebner

Lecture Topics:

1. Introduction: The American Search for Order
2. The Twenties: Isolationism and Internationalism
3. The Challenge of Europe
4. The Washington Conference, 1921-1922
5. The Illusion of Stability: The Kellogg-Briand Pact
6. Challenge of the Dictators
7. Munich to Lend Lease, 1938-1941
8. Crisis in the Far East
9. The Grand Alliance
10. The Fruits of Victory
11. Containment in Europe
12. Challenge of the Far East: Nationalism vs. Communism
13. Global Containment: Indochina and Korea

Midterm

14. Dulles and the Quest for a New Diplomacy
15. Hemispheric Security
16. The Middle East and the Cold War
17. The Defense of Europe
18. The Challenge of de Gaulle
19. Containment in Europe: The Sixties
20. Indochina: The Eisenhower Years
21. The War in Vietnam: The Kennedy-Johnson Years
22. Containment in Crisis
23. Detente: The Nixon-Kissinger Leadership
24. Failure in Vietnam: 1969-1975
25. The Carter Foreign Policies
26. Reagan's Search for Security

History US 338 (2)

<u>Books assigned to all students</u>:

Richard Dean Burns and Edward M. Bennett, eds., DIPLOMATS IN CRISIS: UNITED
   STATES-CHINESE-JAPANESE RELATIONS, 1919-1941 (Regina).
Raymond G. O'Connor, DIPLOMACY FOR VICTORY: FDR AND UNCONDITIONAL SURRENDER
   (Norton).
Adam B. Ulam, THE RIVALS: AMERICA AND RUSSIA SINCE WORLD WAR II (Penguin).
Richard J. Barnet, INTERVENTION AND REVOLUTION (New American Library).
John G. Donovan, THE COLD WARRIORS: A POLICY-MAKING ELITE (Heath).

<u>Reading assignment for the mid-term examination</u>:

Burns and Bennett, DIPLOMATS IN CRISIS. This assignment will be covered in an
   open book examination. Write the essay in a bluebook.
O'Connor, DIPLOMACY FOR VICTORY, entire book.
Ulam, THE RIVALS, pages 3-193.

For the open book examination, write an answer of between 1200 and 1500 words
to <u>one</u> of the following two questions:

In terms of American interests in the Far East, was the United States
justified in maintaining its pro-Chinese, anti-Japanese posture in the decade
before Pearl Harbor?

In terms of Japanese interests in the Orient, was the Tokyo government
justified in maintaining its aggressive posture toward the Asian mainland in
the decade before Pearl Harbor?

<u>Reading assignment for the final examination</u>:

Ulam, THE RIVALS, pages 194-395.
Barnet, INTERVENTION AND REVOLUTION, entire book.
Donovan, THE COLD WARRIORS, entire book.

BROWN UNIVERSITY

AMERICAN FOREIGN POLICY SINCE 1941

History 160/Graduate Level
Spring Term, 1981

Professor Neu
Brown University

I.   Struggle for Survival, 1941-1945

     Feb. 2-6
          Stephen E. Ambrose, Rise to Globalism, Introduction and chapter 1.*
          John Lewis Gaddis, The United States and the Origins of the Cold
              War, 1-173.*
          Thomas G. Paterson, ed., Major Problems in American Foreign Policy
              Since 1914, chapter 7.*
     Feb. 9-13
          Herbert Feis, The Atomic Bomb and the End of World War II, 3-201.*
          Paterson, Major Problems, chapter 8.

II. The Cold War, 1945-1952

     Feb. 16-20
          Gaddis, The United States and the Origins of the Cold War, 174-362.*
          Paterson, Major Problems, chapter 9.

III. The China Tangle, 1941-1952

     Feb. 23-27
          Warren I. Cohen, America's Response to China, chapters 4-6.

IV. The Era of Containment, 1952-1965

     March 2-6
          Ambrose, Rise to Globalism, chapters 5-9.*
          Paterson, Major Problems, chapters 10 and 11.
     March 13
          MIDTERM EXAMINATION - Term essays due
     March 16-20
          Ambrose, Rise to Globalism, chapter 10-11.
          Paterson, Major Problems, chapter 12.
          Arthur M. Schlesinger, Jr.. A Thousand Days, chs. 7-12, 29-34.*

V.   Vietnam and Beyond, 1965-1980

     March 23-27
          John G. Stoessinger, Henry Kissinger and the Anguish of Power, 1-227.*
          Paterson, Major Problems, chapter 14.
     April 6-10
          George Herring, America's Longest War, all of this.*
          Paterson, Major Problems, chapter 13.
     April 13-17
          Ambrose, Rise to Globalism, chapter 13.
          William B. Quandt, Decade of Decisions: American Policy toward the
              Arab-Israeli Conflict, 1967-1976, 1-300.*
     April 20-24
          George F. Kennan, The Cloud of Danger, 3-234.*
          Ambrose, Rise to Globalism, chapters 14-15.

2

Reading Period Assignment

Read one of the following books:

Ernest R. May, "Lessons" of the Past*
George W. Ball, Diplomacy for a Crowded World*
John Lewis Gaddis, Russia, the Soviet Union, and the United States*
Francis Fitzgerald, Fire in the Lake*

You may, however, choose another book from among those I put on the board before lecture, if it will relate better to the central themes of your final exam.

May 18   FINAL EXAMINATIONS DUE

*These books may be purchased in the bookstore.

Discussion Sections

Each Friday the class will divide into discussion sections, which will meet at 10:00 and 11:00.

Examinations

You must write either a midterm, an in-class essay exam, or a term essay, a 10 page typed interpretative essay based on some reading beyond the course syllabus. The final exam will be a take-home and will cover the whole of the term. Prior to the final I will hand out instructions and list of questions.

Course Grade

The midterm or term essay counts for 40 percent of the grade, the final exam for 60 percent.

Late Papers

Any term essay or final exam turned in late--without my permission--will be marked down one notch in the grading scale for every 24 hours that it is late. Thus an A exam turned in 24 hours late would become an A-, 48 hours late a B+, and so on. If a paper is late, it must be given to the departmental secretary so that she can note its time of arrival.

Incompletes

I will not grant any incompletes in the course unless you have a medical excuse from the University Health Service. It must be delivered to me prior to the due date of the final examination.

QUEENS UNIVERSITY, ONTARIO, CANADA

HISTORY 854

United States Foreign Relations in the Twentieth Century

Professor Geoffrey S. Smith   1983-1984

Course Description: The threat of nuclear war in the post-1945
era and disenchantment with United States involvement in Vietnam have
led growing numbers of historians to analyze more critically the
basic assumptions of American foreign policy. This reassessment,
which began in the late 1950s, has resulted in hundreds of "revisionist"
monographs and articles challenging traditional interpretations of
American diplomacy. Historians have moved from the study of an elite
cadre of decision makers and themes of power and conflict and the
motivation of ruling groups, to a consideration of social problems that
nurtured animosities across frontiers, the importance of public opinion,
nationalism, racism, ethnicity, religion, and various intangibles in
confrontations between societies. The historian of American foreign
relations is now often a synthesizer of materials from diplomatic,
political, economic, intellectual, cultural, psychological, and
social sources.

History 854 will involve students with these and other themes while
analyzing the history and historiography of U.S. foreign relations from
the 1890s to the present time. The course is designed not only to make
you more familiar than before with the ideas, themes, interpretations,
and factual content of American diplomatic history, but also to
acquaint you with the scholarly literature and major intellectual
problems related to the field. You are, in addition, expected to gain
some understanding of the problems and techniques of historical and
social science research; to learn to think critically as an historian;
and to engage in analytical research on some topic within the field.
it is hoped that this will provide an understanding of the complexity
of the subject, as well as aiding you in developing further important
intellectual skills--reading for content, developing good writing habits,
and refining your ability to think critically and work independently.

During the year we shall also discuss general topics such as:

  1. Problems of writing, but particularly of history
  2. The task of the historian
  3. The special problems of the American diplomatic historian
  4. The use of government publications
  5. The value of bibliographical guides
  6. The weighing of evidence and sources
  7. The value of documentation and bibliographies
  8. the nature and use of interpretation
  9. The importance of structure and theme
 10. History and the social sciences
 11. The nature of primary sources, especially manuscripts
 12. The use of libraries
 13. The need and use of foreign languages
 14. The importance of other fields, such as philosophy or literature

<u>Course Mechanics</u>: The assignments listed below will provide the core readings for the first portion of the course, which will encompass the fall term, and a small portion of the winter term. These books are available at the Campus Bookstore, and a few copies of each have been placed on reserve in Douglas Library. A few of the books, and articles are only available on reserve. In addition to the recommended background text, <u>American Foreign Policy: A History Since 1900</u> (Paterson, Clifford, Hagan), textbooks by Thomas A. Bailey, Alexander De Conde, and Robert Ferrell have been placed on reserve for reference purposes.

All students will also be expected to join the Society for Historians of American Foreign Relations (SHAFR), at a modest fee, for the 1983-1984 academic year.

The course is divided into two segments. Beginning with the third week of classes, selected members of the seminar will prepare written reports, which will provide the basis of our discussions. These papers should be typed, from seven-to-ten pages in length, and concise examples of good prose style. If the report is a book review, the student should show familiarity with the author's other writings, as well as having read the work assigned. The review should also discuss the importance of the author as an historian (political scientist, journalist, diplomat, former president or secretary of state, <u>et al</u>), and his/her unique contribution, if any, in terms of interpretation, methodology, synthesis, pioneering effort, or lasting influence. In analyzing the book (or other historical cource), attention should be accorded the scope, organization, quality and type of research, cources used, major points presented, and the importance of the author's interpretation. Where possible, that interpretation should be related briefly to other important interpretations relating to the topic(s) under consideration. If parts of several books, chapters, articles, or documents are read by one student, emphasis should be placed upon points of agreement and disagreement. In all written work, emphasis will be placed upon the student's ability to employ evidence to develop his/her argument in a cogent manner, in addition to his/her clarity in writing.

Topics for seminars during the first segment of the course will be assigned by the second week of classes. Concurrent with a student's preparation of a paper, that student (or those students) will have the responsibility of leading the seminar, by presenting a short oral report (fifteen to twenty minutes) on his/her work for the week. Two or three other students will follow these "keynoters," in the capacity of commentator-critics. The latter will briefly (five-to-ten minutes) reflect upon their understanding of, and conclusions drawn from, the readings, as well as presenting observations about the strengths and weaknesses of the presentations of the "keynoters." Rebuttals and general discussion will follow. We want these sessions to be lively, insightful, and constructive. I feel strongly that far from being evil themselves, arguments and disagreement among well-informed and thoughtful people comprise the foundation of intellectual development.

Completed short papers will fall due on the Friday following the Monday seminar in which the keynoter(s) made his/her presentation (papers will also be accepted any time that week). Each student must write two short papers (and lead two seminars), with an option to do a third paper and seminar. Each student shall also serve as a commentator on at least two occasions.

Assignments: Supplementary reading lists will be provided on a weekly basis, while readings may also be added to the core list during the course of the year.

Week Two (September 26): The Nature of the History of United States Foreign Relations --

   Alexander DeConde, American Diplomatic History in Transformation
        (1976)
   _____, "What's Wrong With American Diplomatic
        History" (1969) -- reserve
   Laurence Evans, "The Dangers of Diplomatic History" (1970) --
        reserve
   Thomas J. McCormick, "The State of American Diplomatic History"
        (1970) -- reserve
   _____, "Drift or Mastery? A Corporatist Synthesis
        for American Diplomatic History" (1982) -- reserve
   Ernest R. May, "The Decline of Diplomatic History" (1971) -- reserve
   Norman A. Graebner, "The State of Diplomatic History" (1973)
        -- reserve
   Richard W. Leopold, "The History of U.S. Foreign Policy: Past,
        Present and Future" (1977) -- reserve
   David S. Patterson, "What's Wrong (and Right) with American
        Diplomatic History" (1978) -- reserve
   Jerald A. Combs, American Diplomatic History: Two Centuries
        of Changing Interpretations (1983) -- reserve

Week Three (October 3): An Era of Transformation, 1865-1900 --

   Robert L. Beisner, From the Old Diplomacy to the New, 1865-1900
        (1975)
   _____, "Change and Constancy in American Foreign
        Affairs" (1976) -- reserve
   Michael Roskin, "Pearl Harbor to Vietnam: Shifting Generational
        Paradigms and Foreign Policy" (1974) -- reserve
   David A. Hollinger, "T.S. Kuhn's Theory of Science and its
        Implications for History" (1973) -- reserve
   James A. Field, Jr., "American Imperialism: The 'Worst Chapter'
        in Almost Any Book" (1978) -- reserve

Week Four (October 17): From Theodore Roosevelt to Woodrow Wilson --

   Frederick W. Marks III, Velvet on Iron: The Diplomacy of
        Theodore Roosevelt (1979)

Eugene P. Trani, "Cautious Warrior: Theodore Roosevelt and the
Diplomacy of Activism" in Merli and Wilson, Makers of
American Diplomacy (1974)
Helen D. Kahn, "Willard Straight and the Great Game of Empire,"
in Merli and Wilson
Richard M. Abrams, "United States Intervention Abroad: The First
Quarter Century" (1974) -- reserve
Robert E. Osgood, Ideals and Self-Interest in America's Foreign
Relations: The Great Transformation of the Twentieth
Century (1964), pp. ix - 222 (highly recommended)

Week Five (October 24): War and Peace, 1914-1921 --

Ross Gregory, The Origins of American Intervention in the First
World War (1971)
_____, "To Do Good in the World: Woodrow Wilson and
America's Mission," in Merli and Wilson
N. Gordon Levin, Woodrow Wilson and World Politics: America's
Response to War and Revolution (1970)
Robert E. Osgood, Ideals and Self-Interest in America's Foreign
Relations, pp. 223-304 (highly recommended)

Week Six (October 31): The 1920s and 1930s --

Robert E. Osgood, Ideals and Self-Interest in America's Foreign
Relations, complete
Charles DeBenedetti, "Peace Was His Profession: James T. Shotwell
and American Internationalism," in Merli and Wilson
William Kamman, "Henry L. Stimson: Republican Internationalist,"
in Merli and Wilson

Week Seven (November 7): The Coming of World War II --

Bruce M. Russett, No Clear and Present Danger: A Skeptical
View of the U.S. Entry into World War II (1972)
Geoffrey S. Smith, To Save a Nation: American Countersubversives,
the New Deal, and the Coming of World War II (1973) --
reserve
_____, "Isolationism, the Devil, and the Advent of
the Second World War" (1982) -- reserve
Russell D. Buhite, "The Open Door in Perspective: Stanley K.
Hornbeck and American Far Eastern Policy," in Merli and Wilson
Theodore A. Wilson and Richard D. McKinzie, "The Masks of Power:
Franklin D. Roosevelt and the Conduct of American Diplomacy,"
in Merli and Wilson (emphasize pre-war)

Week Eight (November 14): The Diplomacy of the Second World War --
Part I/Europe --

> John Lewis Gaddis, The United States and the Origins of the Cold
> War, 1941-1947 (1972), pp. 1-197
> Wilson and McKinzie, "Masks of Power," in Merli and Wilson,
> complete
> Vojtech Mastny, Russia's Road to the Cold War: Diplomacy, Warfare
> and the Politics of Communism, 1941-1945 (1979)

Week Nine (November 21): The Diplomacy of the Second World War --
Part II/Asia --

> Akira Iriye, Power and Culture: The Japanese-American War,
> 1941-1945 (1981)
> Christopher Thorne, Allies of a Kind: The United States, Britain,
> and the War Against Japan, 1941-1945 (1978)

Week Ten (November 28): The Origins of the Cold War --

> John Lewis Gaddis, The United States and the Origins of the
> Cold War, complete
> _____, "The Emergent Post-Revisionist Synthesis
> on the Origins of the Cold War" (1983) (with comments by
> Lloyd Gardner, Lawrence Kaplan, Warren Kimball, and Bruce
> Kuniholm) -- reserve
> _____, Strategies of Containment: A Critical
> Appraisal of Postwar United States National Security
> Policy (1982), to p. 53
> Gregg Herken, The Winning Weapon: The Atomic Bomb in the Cold
> War, 1945-1950 (1982)
> Frank Merli and Theodore Wilson (eds.), Makers of American
> Diplomacy, pp. 189-284 (essays on Harry Truman, Dean
> Acheson, and George Kennan).
> Geoffrey S. Smith, "'Harry, We Hardly Know You': Revisionism,
> Politics, and Diplomacy, 1945-1954," (1976) -- reserve
> Arthur M. Schlesinger, Jr., "The Cold War Revisited" (1979) --
> reserve

Recommended:

> Thomas G. Paterson, On Every Front: The Making of the Cold
> War (1979)
> Thomas H. Etzold and John Lewis Gaddis (eds.), Containment:
> Documents on American Policy and Strategy, 1945-1950 (1978)
> Ralph Levering, The Cold War, 1945-1972 (1982)
> Alexander DeConde (ed.), Encyclopedia of American Foreign Policy:
> George C. Herring, "The Cold War" I
> Barton Bernstein, "Containment" I
> Walter LaFeber, "The Truman Doctrine" III

Week Eleven (December 5): The Cold War to 1953 --

John Lewis Gaddis, Strategies of Containment, pp. 54-126
Walter LaFeber, America, Russia, and the Cold War, 1945-1980
(1980), chs. 1-6
George C. Herring, America's Longest War: The United States
and Vietnam, 1950-1975 (1979), (to p. 42)
Ernest R. May, "Lessons of the Past": The Use and Misuse of
History in American Foreign Policy (1975), (to p. 86)
Nancy Bernkopf Tucker, Patterns in the Dust: Chinese-American
Relations and the Recognition Controversy, 1949-1950 (1983)

Week Twelve (January 9): Eisenhower and Kennedy Foreign Policy --

John Lewis Gaddis, Strategies of Cotnainment, pp. 127-236
Walter LaFeber, America, Russia, and the Cold War (to mid-
chapter ten)
George C. Herring, America's Longest War, pp. 43-107
Robert A. Divine, Eisenhower and the Cold War (1981)
Ronald Steel, "Two Cheers For Ike" (1981) -- reserve
Frank Merli and Theodore Wilson (eds.), Makers of American
Diplomacy (essays on John Foster Dulles and John F. Kennedy)

Week Thirteen (January 16): The United States in Vietnam (Johnson-Nixon) --

John Lewis Gaddis, Strategies of Containment, pp. 237-358
(emphasize 237-273)
Walter LaFeber, America, Russia and the Cold War, 1945-1975,
finish
Francis FitzGerald, Fire in the Lake: The Vietnamese and the
Americans in Vietnam (1972)
George C. Herring, America's Longest War: The United States in
Vietnam, 1950-1975, pp. 108-288
Ernest R. May, "Lessons of the Past," pp. 87-190
Frank J. Merli and Theodore A. Wilson (eds.), Makers of American
Diplomacy from Theodore Roosevelt to Hennry Kissinger
(essays on J.W. Fulbright and Henry Kissinger)
Marilyn B. Young, "Revisionists Revised: The Case of Vietnam"
-- reserve
Peter Marin, "Coming to Terms With Vietnam" -- reserve
Tim O'Brien, Going After Cacciato (1978)

Week Fourteen (January 23): Looking Backward --

James C. Thomson, Jr., Peter W. Stanley, and John C. Perry,
Sentimental Imperialists: The American Experience in
East Asia (1979)
Barry Rubin, Paved With Good Intentions: The American
Experience and Iran (1981)

Research essay: The second portion of the course, beginning in late
January will be occupied with the preparation and writing of research
essays. These essays will centre upon important themes in the history
and historiography of twentieth century American foreign relations.
Each essay must adhere to high standards of historical scholarship,
must be written in competent, if not graceful English prose, and must
be original in its research, analysis, or interpretation. Original
materials should be stressed in research and each essay should have a
clear and unifying theme. The essay should represent your best
intellectual and literary effort. The essay should be about twenty-
five (25) typewritten pages in length, including footnotes and
annotated bibliography.

Procedure: The second portion of the course will be run on a tutorial
basis, with each student expected to confer with me at least once
every two weeks during the winter term. At these meetings you will be
expected to report on your progress, present synopses of your
research, and discuss problems that you have encountered. We shall
meet as a full seminar two or three times during the term, probably in
April, when each student will present a resume of his/her work to
date, an outline of major hypotheses, and an annotated bibliography of
the most salient primary and secondary sources consulted. The resumes
should be from four-to-six pages in length, typewritten, and
reproduced for members of the seminar.

Suggested essay areas: Research papers might centre upon such areas
as the following, with more specificity, according to student interests.
Topics are very negotiable.

    Ideals and Self-Interest in 20th Century American Foreign Relations
    The Spanish-American War: A Great Aberration?
    Theodore Roosevelt and American Foreign Policy
    U.S. Intervention in Latin America: Imperialism or Strategic
        Necessity?
    The Great Rapprochement: The United States and England, 1895-1914
    Public Opinion and United States Foreign Policy
    The United States and the Open Door "Policy"
    American Images of China in the Twentieth Century
    American Images of Japan in the Twentieth Century
    The United States and World War I: Wrong-headed Idealism?
    Woodrow Wilson and Latin America
    The United States and the Bolshevik Revolution
    Culture and Diplomacy
    Force and Diplomacy
    Woodrow Wilson and the League of Nations: A Great Betrayal?
    American Business and Foreign Policy during the Inter-war Years
    The Origins and Significance of the "Good Neighbor" Policy
    Isolationism during the 1930s: Its Character and Impact
    Pacifism during War
    The United States and Germany, 1933-1941
    Pearl Harbor
    Franco-American Relations during World War II
    American Failure in China, 1943-1951
    Containment: Shibboleth or Shield?

The Diplomacy of Atomic Power
The Origins of the Cold War
The Election of 1948: Politics and Diplomacy
Foreign Policy and McCarthyism
The Yalta Conference
The Korean War: Civil-Military Relations & the Problem of
     Miscalculation
Vietnam: Calculated Policy or Historical Accident?
"New Left" Revisionism--Distortion or Illumination?
The United States and the Middle East since World War II
The Tragedy of Lyndon Johnson
The United States and Latin America since World War II
The "Nixon Doctrine" in Historical Perspective

Marks: Students will be evaluated on the basis of the papers
written during the first part of the course; contribution to seminar;
performance during tutorials; and second-term research essay. There
are no written mid-terms or written final examinations in History 854.

Office Hours: My office house are on Fridays, 9:30 to noon, in
Watson 226, but I will make appointments at any mutually convenient
time. I am always pleased to see you.

UNIVERSITY OF PITTSBURGH

HISTORY 161

Fall Term, 1984   Professor Peter Karsten

WAR AND THE MILITARY IN AMERICAN LIFE

This course is concerned with two different phenomena;
(1) the roles military (and anti-military) systems play in
international and national affairs, and in the economic,
social, and cultural life of the U.S.   (2) the effect of
wars on American systems (ethnic or economic groups, the
family, the individual, the economy, politics, etc.). The
first week is designed to acquaint the student with earlier
military systems and war codes as an introduction to the
American experience.

The course is not concerned with battles, tactics,
command, or strategy (except inasmuch as these facets of the
military relate to the primary questions). It is concerned
with: The Social origins of military personnel, the process
of value inculcation, inter-and intra-service tensions, the
relations of the military to other national elites; the
change, or absence of change, resulting from warfare,
military occupation, etc.

The course is organized chronologically, but also
topically, with the format varying from lecture, to pro-
seminar, to discussion with the typical meeting being a
mixture of all three. Students are expected to write brief
(1 page) answers to questions that will be distributed on
about every fifth meeting; these questions are designed to
help you focus on the implications of each of the assigned
readings and to relate each of the readings to the ongoing
class discussions and issues. Students are also expected
either to take a mid-term and a final exam or to conduct a
research project or participate in a group research project.
All such research project alternatives to the exams must be
discussed with and approved by Professor Karsten by the end
of the first month.

You are not expected to read all of the articles and
chapters recommended for each meeting, but you will be expected to read at least two articles or chapters in preparation for each meeting.

At the Book Center, you will find:

>Peter Karsten, ed.   The Military in America

>Morris Janowitz   The Professional Soldier
>(recommended only)

>Marcus Cunliffe   Soldiers and Civilians

>Walter Millis   Arms and Men

My Soldiers and Society can be acquired
directly from the publisher. There are
approximately 35 articles or chapters on
reserve at the Hillman Library Reserve
Book Room (RBR). For full citations of
these see pp. 5, 6, 7 and 8.

DATE	TENTATIVE TITLE OF MEETING	RECOMMENDED READING
September 6	Introduction: Military Systems and Society	Peter Karsten, "Demilitarizing Military History" Military Affairs (Fall, 1972); Kurt Lang, Military Institutions and the Sociology of War; and Stanislav Andreski, Military Organizations and Society
September 11	Primitive, Ancient, Feudal, and Early Modern Military Systems	Alfred Vagts, A History of Militarism, pp. 1-74; Divale and Newcomb essays (RBR)
September 13	Anti-Military Impulses and the Laws of War	Karsten, Law, Soldiers, and Combat, chapter 1, and Schmandt essay (RBR)

DATE	TENTATIVE TITLE OF MEETING	RECOMMENDED READING
September 18	The Colonial Experience: Militia Systems and Volunteers in Different Settings	Bronner, Breen, Wheeler, Anderson, Buffington essays (RBR); Shy essay (Karsten), pp. 3-14)
September 20	War of Independence: Recruitment, Combat and Effects of Service and War	Lender and Benton essays and documents (Karsten pp. 15-44, 57-69); Shy essay (RBR); Kaplan, Middlekauff, Stiverson and Papenfuse essays (RBR); Millis, chapter 1, parts 1,2, & 3
September 25	The Military of the Early Republic (1783-1845): Recruitment and Role	Cunliffe, Soldiers and Civilians, chapters 4, 5 and 9; Millis. Chaper 1, parts 4 and 5; Karsten, Naval Aristocracy, chapters 1-3, 5; McKee essay (RBR); Kohn and Skelton essay; (Karsten, pp. 45-56, 73-110); Herman Melville, White Jacket
October 2	Pacifism and Militarism in the Early Republic	Cunliffe, chapters 2, 3, 6, 7, 10 and 11; Merle Curti, The American Peace Crusade
October 4	The Mexican and Civil Wars; Crisis of Conscience, Recruitment, Morale, Combat and the Effects of Service and War	Hitchcock, Coulter, Maslowski, and Lonn readings; (Karsten, pp. 111-116; 125-157); T. H. Williams, Kerby, Levine, Cain, Bowen, Earnhart essay (RBR); Millis, chapter 2; Ph. Paluden, Victims

DATE	TENTATIVE TITLE OF MEETING	RECOMMENDED READING
October 9	The Army of the "New Empire" (1865-1915): Changing Missions and Service Rivalries	Radabaugh, Gates and Hacker essays (RBR) Hyman, Dearing, Cooper, Leonard, and Karsten essays, (Karsten, pp. 158-183, 194-226, 264-269); Start Millis, chapter 3
October 11	The Navy and the "New Empire": Career Anxieties and New Missions	Karsten, Naval Aristocracy, chapter 4, 6-8; B. Adams essay (RBR); and Millis, chapter 3
October 16	Civilian Militarism in the Fin de Siecle	Mallan reprint; Lutzker, Karsten (Roos and Mahan), McClelland and James essays (RBR); Holmes reading (Karsten, pp. 184-193); G. Linderman, Mirror of War, chapter 3
October 18	The Music of War and the Military	Tape recording and songs by "the ol' perfessor"
October 23	MIDTERM EXAM	
October 25	World War I: Localism, Cosmopolitanism and Modern War	Davis, Cuff and Koistinen (WWI) essays (RBR); Millis, chapter 4; Chambers and White essays (Karsten, pp. 275-314); William March, Company K; S. Cooperman, World War I and The American Novel
October 30	Between the Wars: Interservice Rivalries and Modernization	Green, Morton and Koistinen (Between Wars) essays (RBR); Karsten, pp. 315-316

DATE	TENTATIVE TITLE OF MEETING	RECOMMENDED READING
November 1	World War II: Morale, Combat and Ethics	B. Mauldin, Up Front; S. L. A. Marshall and Gertch essays (Karsten, pp. 333-359); R. Shaffer essay (RBR); Millis, chapter 5
November 6	Nuclear Weapons and the "New Military": Selective Serice, Trainfire, the "Whiz Kids" and enterservice Rivalries	Vandergrift and Karsten readings (Karsten, pp. 363-382); P. Hammond, Supercarriers and B-36's; I. L. Horowitz, ed., Rise and Fall of Project Camelot (RBR); Millis chapter 6; Wubben, Wamsley, Spindler, and Davis-Dolbcare essays (RBR)
November 8	Integration and Race Relations, 1862-1983	Fendrich and Moskos essays (RBR); Art Barbeau, The Unknown Soldiers; R. Dalfiume, Deseg. of U.S. Army
November 13	"The Selling of the Pentagon" (Film)	Palmer essay (Karsten, pp. 383-397)
November 15	The Effects of Military Service and War, I: Recruitment, Training and Combat	Karsten, Soldiers and Society (RBR), pp. 2-171
November 20	Effects...., II: Homecoming, Veterans Status and Effects of War on Society	Karsten, Soldiers and Society (RBR), pp. 172-end; Somit, Tannenhaus and Browning essays (RBR)

DATE	TENTATIVE TITLE OF MEETING	RECOMMENDED READING
November 27	"Obedience" (Film) (The Milgram Experiement)	Brody-Rappaport, Mantell, Phillips, Cockerham, Lizotte-Bordua, Toch, and Berger-Karsten essays (RBR)
November 29	Vietnam and Combat Behavior	Savage-Gabriel and Kelman-Laurence essays (Karsten, pp. 399-455); Karsten, Law, Soldiers and Combat, chapter 2; S. Hersh, Mylai 4; Kinnard essay (RBR); J. Webb, Fields of Fire
December 4	The Modern Military and The Future of The Military in America	Handout: Ladinsky essay (Karsten, pp. 456-482), Smernoff, Ginsburgh, Deininger and Corson essays (RBR); Karsten, Law, Soldiers and Combat, chapter 3; Millis, chapter 8

Allen Davis, "Welfare, Reform, and World War I,"
American Quarterly Review, (1967), 516ff

J.S. Radebaugh, "Custer Explores the Black Hills,
1874," Military Affairs (1962-63), 162-170

Brooks Adams, "War as the Ultimate Form of Economic
Competition," U.S. Naval Institute Proceedings
(1903), 829-881

Douglas Kinnard, "The Vietnam War in Retrospect:
The Army Generals' Views." Journal of Political
and Military Sociology (1976), 17-28

Don Bowen, "Guerilla War in Western Missouri,
1862-65: Historical Extensions of The Relative
Deprivation Hypothesis," Comp. Studies in Soc.
and History (1977), 30-51

F. W. Anderson, "Why Did Colonial New Englanders
Make Bad Soldiers? Contractual Principles and
Military Conduct During the Seven Years War,"
William and Mary Quarterly XXXVIII (1981), 395-417

Marvin Cain, "A 'Face of Battle' Needed: An Assess-
ment of Motives and Men in Civil War Historiography,"
Civil War History, XXVIII (1982), 5-27

John Gates, "The Alleged Isolation of U.S. Army
Officers in the Late 19th Century," Parameters, X
(1982), 32-45

Gerald Linderman, "The War and the Small-Town
Community," chapter 3 of The Mirror of War

Peter Levine, "Draft Evasion in the North during
the Civil War, 1863-65," Journal of American History,
46 (1981), 816-34

Lizotte and Bordua, "Military Socialization, Child-
hood Socialization and Veteran's Firearms Ownership,"
Journal of Military and Pol. Sociology, VIII (1980),
243-56

Peter Karsten, "Consent and the American Soldier"
Parameters (1982), 42-49

Peter Karsten, "Ritual and Rank," Armed Forces and
Society (1983), 427-440

ARTICLE CITATIONS

P. Karsten, Law, Soldiers, and Combat

R. Schmandt, "The 4th Crusade and the Just-War Theory," Catholic Historical Review, LXI (191-221)

P. Karsten, "Demilitarizing Military History,' Military Affairs, October 1972

A. Buffington, "The Puritan View of War," Colonial Society of Mass. Publications, XXVIII (1930-33), 67-86

E. Bronner, "Quakers and Non-Violence in PA.", PA. History 1968, 1-22

W. Benton, "PA. Revolutionary Officers and the Federal Constitution," PA. History, 1964, 419-435

R. Kohn, "Inside History of Newburgh Conspiracy," William and Mary Quarterly, April 1970, 186-220

R. Kohn, "Creation of American Military Establishment, 1783-1802," typescript

P. Maslowski, "Study of Morale in Civil War Soldiers," Military Affairs" 1970, pp. 122-126

R. Kerby, "Why The Confederacy Lost," Review of Politics, summer, 1973, 326-345

B. C. Hacker, "U.S. Army as a National Police Force, 1877-1898," Military Affairs, 1966, pp. 25555ff

T. Leonard, "Red, White and Army Blue," American Quarterly, 1974, 1976-190

P. Karsten, "Armed Progressives: The Army" in J. Israel, ed., Building the Organizational Society, pp. 196-97, 216-232

Stiverson and Papenfuse, "General Smallwoods Recruits," William and Mary Quarterly, January 1973, 117-132

William James, "The Moral Equivalent of War," in
St. Lynd, ed., Non-violence in America, 135-150

P. Koistinen, "Military-Industrial Complex...The
Interwar Years," Journal of American History
(1970), 812ff.

G. Spindler, "Doolittle Board and Cooptation in
Army." Social Forces, 1951, 305-310

P. Karsten, "The American Democ. Citizen Soldier,"
Military Affairs, XXX (1966)

E. Berger, et. al., "ROTC, Mylai and the Volunteer
Army," Foreign Policy, 1971, pp. 135-160

R. Middlekauff, "Why Men Fought in the American
Revolution," Huntington Library Quarterly,
XLIII (Spring, 1980)

L. Dexter, "Congressmen and the Making of Military
Policy," in New Perspectives on the House of
Representatives, ed. Robert Peabody, pp. 175-194

R. Ginsburgh, "Challenge to Military Professionalism,"
Foreign Affairs, 1964, pp. 255-268

H. Browning, et. al., "Income and Veteran Status,"
American Sociological Review, February 1973, 74-85

N. Phillips, "Militarism and Grass-Roots Involvement in Mil-Ind. Complex," Journal of Conflict
Res., December 1973, 625-655

H. Toch, et. al., "Readiness to Perceive Violence,"
British J. of Psychology, 1961, Volume 52, 389-393

W. Corson, "Toward a Concept ofMilitary Domestic
Action,' typescript

Ens. Deininger, "The Career Officer as Existential
Hero," U.S. Naval Institute Proceedings
(November 1970), 18-22

A. Yarmolinsky, "The Military Establishment,"
Foreign Policy, 1 (1971), 78-97

H. Earnhart, "Commutation," Civil War History, IXX,
(June, 1966), 132-142

C. Moskos, "Racial Integration in Armed Forces,'
American Journal of Sociology, September 1966, 132-148

Thomas Palmer, "Why We Fight': A Study of Indoctrination Activities in the Armed Forces," unpublished
paper for 1971 I.U.S.A.F.S. conference

Barry Smernoff - Military Technology in the 1980's,
Hudson Institute Paper 1973

John Shy, "The American Revolution" The Military
Conflict as a Revolutionary Conflict in Essay on
the American Revolution, ed. St. Kurtz and James
Huston, pp. 121-156

Nancy Stein, "U.S. Army School for Scoundrels,"
NACLA VIII (1974) 24-27

William Cockerham, "Selective Socialization:
Airforce Training as Status Passage," Journal
of Political and Military Sociology (Fall, 1973),
215-229

Louis Morton, "Army and Marines on The China
Station," Pacific Historical Review (1960), 51-74

Ron Shaffer, "American Military Ethnics in WWII:
The Bombing of German Civilians," Journal of
American History (September 1980)

Roger Little, "Buddy Relations and Combat Performance," in The New Military ed. Morris
Janowitz (1964), 195-223

Kenneth Dolbeare and James Davis, "A Social Profile
of Local Draft Board Members: The Case of Wisconsin,"
and Gary Wamsley, "Decision-making in Local Boards:
(the case of Pittsburgh) both in Wamsley, ed.,
Selective Service

W. Lloyd Warner, "The Symbolic Relations of the
Dead and the Living," in The Living and the Dead,
248-279

Mantell, "Doves vs. Hawks," Psychology Today,
(September 1974)

N. Lutzker, "The Pacifist as Militarist, A
Critique of the American Peace Movement, 1898-1914"
unpublished MSS.

H. H. Wubben, "American POWs in Korea,"
American Quarterly (1972), 3-19

T. Breen, "English Origins and New World Development: The Case of the Conenanted Militia, 17th.
C. Mass." Past and Present (1972), 74-96

D. McClelland, "Love and Power: The Psychological
Signals of War," Psychology Today (January 1975)
44ff.

Brody and Rappaport, "Violence and Vietnam,"
Human Relations, XXVI, No. 6, 735-52

P. Karsten, "The Nature of 'Influence': Roosevelt,
Mahan and the Concept of Sea Power," American
Quarterly (Fall, 1971), 585-600

S. Kaplan, "Rank and Status Among Mass. Cont. Line
Offs." American Historical Review, LVI (1950-51),
318-326

PRINCETON UNIVERSITY

Department of History

Fall Term, 1983   HISTORY 411

Prof. James McPherson
Prof. John Murrin
Prof. Richard Challener

WAR AND SOCIETY IN THE MODERN WORLD

History 411 will meet on Thursday afternoons from 1:30 to 4:00 p.m. in 230 Dickinson.

Course requirements: Two book reviews and a 15-20 page term paper.

The following assigned books are available for purchase at the University Store:

Adams, Michael, Our Masters the Rebels: A Speculation on the Union Military Failure in the East, 1861-1865 (Hardcover, Harvard, 1978)

Brodie, Bernard and Fawn, From Crossbow to H-Bomb (Indiana, 1973)

Connelly, Thomas and Archer Jones, The Politics of Command: Factions and Ideas in Confederate Strategy

Donald, David, ed., Why the North Won the Civil War (Collier, 1962)

Earle, Edward Mead, Makers of Modern Strategy (Princeton, 1943)

Ferro, Marc, The Great War 1914-1918 (Routledge and Kegan, 1973)

Fussell, Paul, The Great War and Modern Memory (Oxford, 1977)

Howard, Michael, War in European History

Hubbell, John, ed., Battles Lost and Won: Essays from "Civil War History" (Greenwood, 1975)

Keegan, John, The Face of Battle (Random, 1977)

Keegan, John, Six Armies in Normandy (Penguin, 1982)

McWhiney, Grady and Perry Jamieson, Attack and Die: Civil War Military Tactics and Southern Heritage

Ropp, Theodore, War in the Modern World (MacMillan, 1962)

Shy, John, A People Numerous and Armed (Oxford, 1977)

Weigley, Russell, The American Way of War (Indiana, 1977)

Weigley, Russell, The Partisan War (University of South Carolina, 1978)

Week of September 12   Introductory Themes

Assigned Readings

Howard, War in European History, Chapters 1-3
Ropp, War in the Modern World, Chapters 1-4
Brodie and Brodie, From Crossbow to H-Bomb, pp. 7-123

Week of September 19   Gunpowder and the Military Revolution

Assigned Readings

Keegan, The Face of Battle, Chapters 1 and 2
Earle, Makers of Modern Strategy, Chapters 1 (Machiavelli) and 2 (Vauban)
*Michael Robert, Essays in Swedish History, Chapters 3 and 7
*Geoffrey Parker, The Army of Flanders and the Spanish Road, Introduction,
    Chapters 1, 5, 7-10
*Geoffrey Parker, "The Military Revolution, A Myth", Journal of Modern History
    Vol. 48 (1976)

Additional Readings

J. F. Guilmartin, Gunpowder and Galleys (Cambridge)
Andre Corvisier, Armies and Societies in Europe
Myron Gutman, War and Rural Life (Princeton)
I.A.A. Thompson, War and Government in Hapsburg Spain
David Chandler, Marlborough as Military Commander (Batsford)

Week of September 26   Of Massacres, Indian Wars and National Traditions

Assigned Readings

Carl Bridenbaugh, Jamestown, 1544-1699 (1980), 10-33
William S. Powell, "Aftermath of the Massacre: The First Indian War, 1622-1632,"
    Virginia Magazine of History and Biography, 66 (1958), 44-75
Allen W. Trelease, Indian Affairs in Colonial New York: The Seventeenth
    Century (1960), 60-85
Francis Jennings, The Invasion of America: Indians, Colonialism, and the
    Cant of Conquest (1975), 202-27
Richard Slotkin, Regeneration through Violence: The Mythology of the
    American Frontier, 1600-1860 (1973), 146-79
Patrick M. Malone, "Changing Military Technology among the Indians of
    Southern New England, 1600-1677," American Quarterly, 25 (1973), 48-63
James Axtell, "The White Indians of Colonial America," William and Mary
    Quarterly, 3rd ser., 32 (1975), 55-88. Also available in his The
    European and the Indian: Essays in the Ethnohistory of Colonial North
    America (1981), 168-206, and in Stanley N. Katz and John M. Murrin (eds.),
    Colonial America: Essays in Politics and Social Development, 3rd edn.
    (1983), 16-47
Daniel K. Richter, "Captives, Furs, and Empires: Warfare and Iroquois Society
    to 1715" (unpublished essay)
F. W. Anderson, "Why Did Colonial New Englanders Make Bad Soldiers? Contractual
    Principles and Military Conduct During the Seven Years' War," William
    and Mary Quarterly, 3rd ser., 38 (1981), 395-417

Thomas L. Purvis, "Colonial Participation in the Seven Years' War, .1755-1763
    (unpublished paper)
John Shy, <u>A People Numerous and Armed: Reflections on the Military Struggle
    for American Independence</u> (1976), 21-34, 225-54

Additional Readings

All of Jennings
All of Slotkin through Daniel Boone
Douglas E. Leach, <u>Flintlock and Tomahawk: New England in King Philip's War</u>,
    (1958)
Stephen S. Webb, The <u>Governors General: The English Army and the Definition
    of the Empire,</u> 1569-1681 (1979)
William Pencak, <u>War, Politics, & Revolution in Provincial Massachusetts</u> (1981)
Guy Fregault, <u>Canada: The War of the Conquest</u> (1969)

Week of October 3   War and Revolution

Assigned Readings

Russell F. Weigley, <u>The American Way of War</u> (1973), 3-55
Shy, <u>People Numerous and Armed</u>, 73-107, 133-224
Neil L. York, "Pennsylvania Rifle: Revolutionary Weapon in a Conventional
    War?" <u>Pennsylvania Magazine of History and Biography</u>, 103 (1979),
    302-24
Earle, Makers of Modern Strategy, 49-74: R. R. Palmer, "Frederick the
    Great, Guibert, Bulow: From Dynastic to National War"
N.H. Gibbs and C.C. Lloyd, "Armed Forces and the Art of War," in <u>The New
    Cambridge Modern History</u>, IX: <u>War and Peace in an Age of Upheaval,
    1793-1830</u>, ed. C.W. Crawley (1965), 60-90 (open reserve)
J.F.C. Fuller, <u>A Military History of the Western World</u> (1954-56) II,
    341-69 (on Valmy)

Additional Readings

Piers Mackesy, <u>The War for America, 1775-1783</u> (1964)
Charles Royster,<u>A Revolutionary People at War: The Continental Army and
    American Character, 1775-1783</u> (1979)
Thomas J. Fleming, <u>1776: Year of Illusions</u> (1975)
Paul H. Smith, <u>Loyalists and Redcoats: A Study in British Revolutionary
    Policy</u> (1964)
Adrian C. Leiby, <u>The Revolutionary War in the Hackensack Valley: The Jersey
    Dutch and the Neutral Ground</u> (1962)
Richard Buel, Jr., <u>Dear Liberty: Connecticuts's Mobilization for the
    Revolutionary War</u> (1980)
Jean-Paul Bertaud , <u>Valmy: la Democratie en armes</u> (1970)
R.R. Palmer, <u>Twelve Who Ruled: The Year of the Terror in the French
    Revolution</u> (1941, 1958)
Samuel F. Scott, <u>The Response of the Royal Army to the French Revolution:
    The Role and Development of the Line Army, 1787-1793</u> (1978)
James Dugan, <u>The Great Mutiny</u> (1965)

Week of October 10. Napoleonic Warfare

Assigned Readings

David Chandler, The Campaigns of Napoleon (1966), either 133-201 (general
    chp. on Napoleon's art of war) or 381-439 (Austerlitz)
Georges Lefebvre, Napoleon, transl. Henry F. Stockhold (1969), I, 214-31
Fuller, Military History of the Western World, II, 370-404 (Trafalgar)
Alfred Vagts, A History of Militarism, Civilian and Military, rev. edn.
    (1959), 104-52
Keegan, Face of Battle, 117-203
Earle, Makers of Modern Strategy, 77-113, 117-54

Additional Readings

Felix Markham, Napoleon (1963)
David Howarth, Trafalgar: The Nelson Touch (1969)
Peter Paret, Yorck and the Era of Prussian Reform, 1807-1815 (1966)
Chandler Campaigns of Napoleon, from Wagram to abdication of 1814
Richard H. Kohn, Eagle and Sword: The Beginnings of the Military Establishment
    in America, 1783-1802 (1975)
Roger H. Brown, The Republic in Peril: 1812 (1964)
Antoine Henri Jomini, The Art of War, transl. G.H. Mandell and W.P. Craighill
    (1862; Greenwood reprint, n.d.)
Carl von Clausewitz, On War, transl. and ed. Michael Howard and Peter
    Paret [1976]

Week of October 17   Strategy and Leadership in the American Civil War

Assigned Readings

Weigley, The American Way of War, chaps. 6-7
David Donald, ed., Why the North Won the Civil War
John Hubbell, ed., Battles Lost and Won: Essays from Civil War History,
    essays no. 1, 4, 9, 12, 14, 15.
Thomas L. Connelly and Archer Jones, The Politics of Command: Factions and
    Ideas in Confederate Strategy, Introduction and chaps. 1-3, 6.

Additional Readings:

T. Harry Williams, Lincoln and His Generals
Herman Hattaway and Archer Jones, How the North Won: A Military History of
    the Civil War
Warren W. Hassler, Jr., Commanders of the Army of the Potomac
Archer Jones, Confederate Strategy from Shiloh to Vicksburg
Thomas L. Connelly, The Marble Man: Robert E. Lee and His Image in American
    Society

Week of October 24   Fall Break

Week of October 31   Culture and Tactics: The American Civil War as a
    Test Case
Michael Adams, Our Masters The Rebels
Grady McWhiney and Perry D. Jamieson, Attack and Die: Civil War
    Tactics and the Southern Heritage

Additional Readings

Bell I. Wiley, The Life of Johnny Reb
Bell I. Wiley, The Life of Billy Yank
Paul D. Escott, After Secession: Jefferson Davis and the Failure of Confederate
    Nationalism
George M. Fredrickson, The Inner Civil War: Northern Intellectuals and the
    Crisis of the Union
Richard S. Brownlee,Gray Ghosts of the Confederacy: Guerrilla Warfare in
    the West, 1861-1865
Virgil Carringon Jones, Gray Ghosts and Rebel Raiders

Week of November 7   From Appomattox to the Marne:Europe and America,
    1865-1914

Assigned Readings

Weigley, The American Way of War, chaps. 8-9
Jay Luvaas, The Military Legacy of the Civil War: The European Inheritance,
    pp. 1-99, 170-233.
G.F.R. Henderson, The Civil War: A Soldier's View. ed. Jay Luvaas, pp. 130-73:
    "Battles and Leaders of the Civil War" (Xerox copy to be provided).
Ropp, War in the Modern World, pp. 177-217
Howard, War in European History, 94-115.
Earle, Makers of Modern Strategy, pp. 172-233, 410-45.

Additional Readings

G.F.R. Henderson, Stonewall Jackson and the American Civil War
J.F.C. Fuller, Grant & Lee: A Study in Personality and Generalship
Basil H. Liddell Hart, Sherman: Soldier, Realists, American
R.D. Challener, The French Theory of the Nation in Arms, 1866-1939 (Columbia)
Michael Howard, The Franc -Prussian War
Bernard Brodie, Seapower in the Machine Age
James L. Abrahamson, America Arms for a New Century: The Making of a Great
    Military Power
Paul M. Kennedy, The War Plans of the Great Powers, 1880-1914
Alfred Vagts,A History of Militarism. Civilian and Military (Parts II and III)
Gordon Craig, The Politics of the Prussian Army
Paul-Marie de la Corce, The French Army: A Military-Political History
Douglas Porch, The March to the Marne: The French Army, 1871-1914
Samuel Williamson, The Politics of Grand Strategy: Britain and France
    Prepare for War, 1904-1914
Walter Goerlitz, History of the German General Staff

Week of November 14   The First World War

Assigned Readings

Keegan, Face of Battle, pp. 204-84
Ferro, The Great War, pp. 49-226
Weigley, American Way of War, pp. 192-222
Brodie and Brodie, Crossbow to H-Bomb, 172-99
Ropp, War in the Modern World, pp. 221-55

Additional Readings

Barbara Tuchman, The Guns of August
Corelli Barnet, The Swordbearers
Gerhard Ritter, The Schlieffen Plan: Critique of a Myth
John Tolane, No Man's Land
Robert Asprey, At Belleau Wood
Frank Vandiver, Black Jack
Elting Morison, Admiral Sims and the Modern American Navy
Arthur Marder, From the Dreadnought to Scapa Flow
Alistair Horne, The Price of Glory: Verdun, 1916
Erich Memarque, All Quiet on the Western Front
Jules Romain, Verdun

Week of November 21   No Meeting: Thanksgiving

Week of November 28 The Interwar Years: Strategy, Theory, Organization

Assigned Readings

Paul Fussell, The Great War and Modern Memory, pp. 1-75
Earle, Makers of Modern Strategy, pp. 306-64 (Ludendorf, Lenin, Trotsky),
(365-87 Maginot and Liddell Hart Stalin) 485-503 (Douhet, Mitchell, Seversky)
Ropp, War in the Modern World, pp. 256-93
Weigley, American Way of War, pp. 223-65
Wesley F. Craven and James Lea Cate, The Army Air Forces in World War II
    Vol I, Plans and Operations, pp. 17-71

Additional Readings

John Wheeler-Bennett, The Nemesis of Power
Barbara Tuchman, Stilwell and the American Experience in China
Alfred F. Hurley, Billy Mitchell: Crusader for Air Power
Bernard Brodie, A Layman's Guide to Naval Strategy
Forest Pogue, George C. Marshall: The Education of a General, 1880-1939
Jeffrey Gunsburg, The French High Command and the Defeat of the West 1940

Also, relevant portions of previously cited volumes by Challener,
    de la Gorce, Craig

Week of December 5   The Second World War

Assigned Readings:

John Keegan, Six Armies in Normandy, pp. 1-142, 183-248, 313-35
Marc Bloch, The Strange Defeat, pp.
Weigley, American Way of War, pp. 269-359
Ronald Lewin, The American Magic, pp.

Additional Reading

Forrest Pogue, George C. Marshall. Organizer of Victory, 1942-45
Omar Bradley and Clay Blair, A General's Life
William Manchester, Goodbye   Darkness
Charles MacDonald, Company Commander
Charles MacDonald, The Battle of the Huertgen Forest
Harold Bond, Return to Cassino
Williamson Murray, Strategy for Defeat: The Luftwaffe, 1933-45
Stephen Ambrose,   The Supreme Commander: The War Years of General Dwight
      D. Eisenhower
Gordon Prange, At Dawn We Slept
John Costello, The Pacific War
J.F.C. Fuller, The Second World War
Samuel Eliot Morison, The Two-Ocean War
Charles F. Romanus and Riley Sunderland, Stilwell's Mission to China
Cornelius Ryan, The Longest Day and A Bridge Too Far
John Toland, The Last 100 Days

Week of January 2   The Beginning of the Atomic Era

Assigned Readings

Jonathan Schell, The Fate of the Earth, pp. 1-96
Hiroshima and Nagasaki, The Physical, Medical and Social Effects of the
      Atomic Bombings
John Keegan, "The Spectre of Conventional War, "Harper's, July, 1983
David Rosenberg, "The Beginnings of Overkill: Nuclear Weapons in American
      Strategy," 1945-1960", International Security, (Spring, 1983)

Additional Reading

Richard Hewlett and Oscar Anderson, The New World
Michael Amrine, The Great Decision: The Secret History of the Atomic Bomb
Lansing Lamont, Day of Trinity
John Hersey, Hiroshima
Gregg Herken, The Winning Weapon: The Atom Bomb in the Cold War, 1945-50
Martin J. Sherwin, A World Destroyed: The Atomic Bomb and the Grand Alliance

UNIVERSITY OF MICHIGAN

HISTORY 366

Twentieth-Century American Wars as Social and Personal Experience

Gerald F. Linderman
3633 Haven Hall
764-6353/971-8562

Course Assistants:

Howard W. Koepp
Thomas W. Collier

Fall Term 1982

Office Hours: Tuesdays 4:15 - 5:45
              and by Appointment

History 366 will examine--via talks, books, films and optional discussion sections--America's wars of the past eighty-five years, with emphasis on those which have engaged this society since 1940.

The stress will fall on individual perceptions of war's purposes and meanings as they are revealed in autobiography and fiction and on the patterns of personal experience in combat as they alter from war to war. In larger historical perspective, the following themes will receive attention: American society's pattern of response to situations of conflict; methods of mobilizing the nation for war; the experience of the homefront; American images of ally and enemy; and the role of technology in altering the nature of war. There will be almost no discussion of tactics or the technical processes of war-making.

The class will meet from 2:00 to 4:00 each Tuesday afternoon and from 2:00 to 3:00 each Thursday afternoon, with Tuesday's second hour devoted principally to film showings. Otherwise, the general format will be that of the lecture, although the instructor asks, and needs, frequent and vigorous student intervention. The Course Assistants will organize discussion sections and will invite the attendance of those who are interested.

There are no history-course prerequisites for History 366.

Required Texts

John Blum et al.	The National Experience, Part II Only, A History of the United States Since 1865, Fifth Edition (Harcourt Brace Jovanovich): Course Textbook
John Blum	Woodrow Wilson and the Politics of Morality (Little Brown)
Philip Caputo	A Rumor of War (Ballantine)
J. Glenn Gray	The Warriors (Harper Torchbook)
David Halberstam	The Best and the Brightest (Fawcett Crest)
Anthony Herbert	Soldier (Cloverleaf)
Steven Jantzen	Hooray for Peace, Hurrah for War (Mentor)
James Jones	WWII (Ballantine)
Erich Remarque	All Quiet on the Western Front (Fawcett)
A.J.P. Taylor	The Second World War (Paragon)

Spanish-American War Course-Pack (available at Dollar-Bill Copying, 611 Church Street, 665-9200).

Class Schedule

First Week

Thursday, September 9
    Introduction
    Reading: Textbook, pages 522-539

Second Week

Tuesday, September 14
    The Spanish-American War: Origins and the Role of William McKinley
    Film: Theodore Roosevelt (Biography Series) (26 minutes)

Thursday, September 16
    The Spanish-American War: Images of Ally and Enemy
    Reading: Spanish-American War Course-Pack

Third Week

Tuesday, September 21
    The Spanish-American War: Theodore Roosevelt and the War of Personal Encounter
    Films: U.S. Neutrality, 1914-1917 (17) and Home Front, 1917-1919 (17)

Thursday, September 23
    World War One: The Period of American Neutrality
    Reading: Blum, Woodrow Wilson and the Politics of Morality; Textbook, pages 587-594

Fourth Week

Tuesday, September 28
    World War One: Woodrow Wilson and American Intervention
    Film: The Yanks Are Coming (52)

Thursday, September 30
    World War One: America at Home
    Reading: Remarque, All Quiet on the Western Front; Textbook, pages 596-605

Fifth Week

Tuesday, October 5
    World War One: The Combat Experience
    Film: Triumph of the Will (English version)

Thursday, October 7
    The Interwar Period
    Reading: Jantzen, Hooray for Peace, Hurrah for War; Textbook, pages 605-620

Sixth Week

Tuesday, October 12
    World War Two: Pearl Harbor
    Film: The Battle of San Pietro (35)

Thursday, October 14
    World War Two: The Mobilization of the Homefront
    Reading: Taylor, The Second World War

Seventh Week

Tuesday, October 19
    World War Two: The Combat Experience
    Film: D-Day (50)

Thursday, October 21
    World War Two: Two Legacies
    Reading: Gray, The Warriors

Eighth Week

Tuesday, October 26	Topic to be Determined
Thursday, October 28	Mid-Term Examination

Ninth Week

Tuesday, November 2
The Development of the Atomic Bomb
Film: The Bomb (World At War Series)

Thursday, November 4
The Cold War I
Reading: Jones, WWII

Tenth Week

Tuesday, November 9
The Cold War II
Film: Night and Fog (32)

Thursday, November 11
The Korean War: Origins
Reading: Herbert, Soldier; Textbook, pages
758-769; 774-780; 796-797

Eleventh Week

Tuesday, November 16
The Korean War: Truman vs. MacArthur
Film: Truman vs. MacArthur (30)

Thursday, November 18
The Korean War: The Combat Experience
Reading: Halberstam, The Best and the Brightest,
pages to be assigned; Textbook, pages 801-802;
812, 826-829

Twelfth Week

Tuesday, November 23
The Black Soldier
Film: The Black Soldier (26)

Thursday, November 25
Thanksgiving
Reading: Halberstam, pages to be assigned;
Textbook, pages 842-853

Thirteenth Week

Tuesday, November 30
The Vietnam War: Origins
Film: Hearts and Minds (112)

Thursday, December 2
The Vietnam War: The Combat Experience
Reading: Caputo, A Rumor of War

Fourteenth Week

Tuesday, December 7
Women and War
Films: The Selling of the Pentagon (52) and
War Without Winners (26)

Thursday, December 9
Nuclear War
Course Summary

<u>**Reading Questions**</u>

<u>**History 366**</u>

<u>**Twentieth-Century American Wars as Social and Personal Experience**</u>

Questions Pertinent to Readings in the Works of Theodore Roosevelt,
Sherwood Anderson, Carl Sandburg and Stephen Crane

1. Theodore Roosevelt is correct in his assumption that preparedness
   averts war, is he not?

2. Why does Theodore Roosevelt believe that a Spanish-American War is
   necessary?

3. Which groups within American society appear to support the drive for
   war with Spain? Which oppose it?

4. What, in Theodore Roosevelt's mind, determines a man's capability as
   a soldier?

5. In what images does Sherwood Anderson perceive the enemy? Are they
   images that convey Spanish strength or weakness?

6. What is the meaning of Carl Sandburg's observation that "Over all of
   us in 1898 was the shadow of the Civil War and the men who fought it
   to the end"?

7. What is the significance of Wiz Brown's reaction to the news that
   Captain McGirr intends to punish him with a dishonorable discharge?
   If you today found yourself in similar trouble, how would you react?

8. What accounts, do you think, for that "hopeless gulf" between Major
   Gates and Private Lige in Stephen Crane's "Virtue in War"?

9. Is it possible to generalize regarding the volunteers' motivation in
   so enthusiastically wishing to fight a war against Spain?

10. What are the characteristics of 1898's army that separate it from
    today's army?

11. What are the basic assumptions about war shared by Roosevelt, Sandburg
    and Anderson? Why are University of Michigan students today likely to
    think those assumptions untenable?

Questions Pertinent to John Morton Blum's <u>Woodrow Wilson and The Politics</u>
<u>of Morality</u>

1. Please read Chapters 1-4 not in order to master the detail of Woodrow
   Wilson's formative period but to attempt to identify any pattern
   which his actions and responses might reveal. If there is such a
   pattern, does it similarly characterize the post-1914 period of his
   life?

2. Responding to the practical necessities of his campaign for the
   governorship of New Jersey, Woodrow Wilson embraces reform measures
   violative of his earlier beliefs. Responding to the practical
   necessities of the 1916 Presidential campaign, he embraces social
   legislation which he had earlier opposed. The view of Woodrow Wilson
   as a moralist is nonsense.

   Please evaluate this contention.

3. If you, with John Morton Blum, believe Woodrow Wilson a moralist,
   of what specifically does his moralism consist when he is confronted
   by situations of daily reality requiring decisions? In domestic
   policy? In foreign policy?

4. Why is Woodrow Wilson's policy of neutrality, 1914-1917, untenable?

5. Why <u>does</u> the United States enter the war in 1917?

6. What results flow from Woodrow Wilson's willingness to sanction
   George Creel's campaign of propaganda?

7. In completing this reading, do you feel a personal affinity for
   Woodrow Wilson? If you feel pulled towards him, on what grounds
   are you drawn? If you are repulsed, on what grounds?

Questions Pertinent to Erich Maria Remarque's <u>All Quiet on the Western Front</u>

1. Whom do Paul Baumer and his friends hold responsible for the war?

2. Why does Paul Baumer aid the enemy soldier whom he has wounded?

3. Paul Baumer and his friends believe--do they not?--that chance will determine their fates. If so, why do they strive to survive? And if they truly wished to survive, why would they not revolt against participation in the war?

4. What are the major assumptions that separate Paul Baumer from those who remain at home?

5. Are we convinced of the inevitability of Paul Baumer's death? In what ways?

6. How does the experience of this war differ from that of 1898? And to what degree is the 1914-1918 experience as set out in this book the American experience?

Questions Pertinent to Steven Jantzen's Hooray for Peace, Hurrah For War

1. Why, do you suppose, crowds gathering in the streets of European capitals
    in July 1914 were so avid for war? And why is it that Cossack peasants
    "gave up their work without a regret and burned to fight the enemy"
    (page 40)?

2. How would you assign culpability for the outbreak of the Great War?

3. What was the American reaction to the opening of hostilities, and how would
    you explain such a response?

4. Why, entering 1915, were Americans "neutral in fact but not in spirit"
    (page 62)?

5. How would the American Government have defended itself against Tirpitz's
    question (page 65): "Why is it that whatever England does seems all right
    to Americans, while they object to anything Germany does, of the same kind?"
    Against his charge that any policy encompassing the despatch of arms and
    provisions to England and not to Germany could not reasonably be called
    neutrality?

6. Was Germany justified in its destruction of the Lusitania?

7. How would you assess Marie Van Vorst's argument (pages 86, 88-89) in favor
    of American participation? She does, after all, possess a first-hand know-
    ledge unavailable to William Jennings Bryan or Eugene Debs, does she not?

8. With so many Americans opposing their government's intervention in the Great
    War, why is it that the anti-war movement is so anemic?

9. Why does Woodrow Wilson pitch at so exalted a level his presentation of
    America's war purposes?

10. The author does little to conceal his admiration of Debs, Emma Goldman,
    conscientious objectors and other dissidents, but cannot one make a strong
    case in defense of those who move to counter such dissent?

11. How would you characterize women's role in the events here described?

12. Why do Wilsonian plans go awry, Wilsonian hopes turn sour?

Questions Pertinent to A.J.P. Taylor's _The Second World War_

1. What does the author believe to have been Hitler's goal, his design
   for achieving it and the degree of his responsibility for the European
   war? Americans at large continue to uphold positions which dispute
   the author's analysis. In such a conflict of views, those of the
   expert should prevail. Please evaluate this assertion.

2. If neither Japan nor the United States wishes war in the Far East, why
   does war erupt there?

3. Do you agree with the author's assertion that the Japanese attack on
   Pearl Harbor was a stroke of military genius?

4. How does it happen that the British and the Americans, in designing
   Hitler's defeat, come to offer antagonistic strategic conceptions?

5. In what ways do the nature and operation of the Axis alliance -- Germany,
   Italy and Japan -- differ from the nature and operation of the Allied
   alliance -- the Soviet Union, Britain and the United States?

6. Hitler was a military genius whose intuitive decisions transcend the
   insufficiently flexible traditionalism of his military chiefs. Hitler
   was a military amateur whose unversed decisions mock Germany's reputation
   for professional military competence of the highest order. With which
   of these positions do you agree? If neither suffices, how would you
   characterize Hitler's military role?

7. A.J.P. Taylor tells us that four leaders made every important decision
   of the war, but his text seems to suggest a supremacy less of Great Men
   than of the momentum of events. The British bomb indiscriminately
   because it is the only manner of fighting still available to them. The
   British launch the Mediterranean campaign because there is nowhere else
   for them to fight. Hitler attacks Russia because there is no other place
   to employ his large army. The German reaction to the North African
   landings requires an intensification of Allied efforts which in turn
   leads to the invasion of Sicily, etc. Why are Allied troops in Sicily
   and Italy? They are there because they are there. Once the Americans
   develop the atomic bomb, they will of course use it. In short, war
   leaders shape events less than they are shaped by them.

   Please comment, with special thought for any junctures at which an
   individual's intervention may have proven decisive.

8. How and where does the German army suffer its decisive defeat?

9. How would you rank the factors that account for America's overwhelming
   military success in World War Two?

10. What is the lesson that World War Two teaches regarding the efficacy of
    strategic bombing? And why -- do you suppose -- Americans fail to learn
    it?

11. Why does not the United States, as its forces liberate nations from
    Axis control, use its military power to advance social reconstruction
    along democratic lines?

12. Do you agree with the author's judgment of Franklin Roosevelt's
    character and intentions? Of Joseph Stalin's character and intentions?

13. Do you accept for yourself A.J.P. Taylor's position that World War Two
    was justified in its aims and successful in accomplishing them; that
    as a result of that war people are happier, freer, more prosperous;
    that it was a just war, a good war?

Questions Pertinent to J. Glenn Gray's The Warriors

1. Why do soldiers who experience combat not immediately flee from it?

2. What are the enduring appeals of war?

3. What, in the author's estimation, is the relationship between war and love? And what is the distinction between comradeship and friendship?

4. Please evaluate this proposition:

    The greater the suffering that a war inflicts, the greater is its power to immunize human beings against the recurrence.

5. What are the elements that induce hatred of the enemy? That diminish hatred?

6. What is the author's prescription for the avoidance of war? Are you persuaded that he here offers a solution?

7. Many of the questions above are rooted in the assumption that the author's experience of one war permits valid generalization regarding war in its generic sense. Is this an assumption that you accept? Do J. Glenn Gray's conclusions, for example, apply with equal force to World War Two and to Vietnam?

8. Is J. Glenn Gray's vision of war compatible with your own? If not, why do you find it either intellectually or emotionally alien?

Questions Pertinent to James Jones' <u>WWII</u>

1. How would you proceed to evaluate James Jones' assertions that the attack on Pearl Harbor was not, as some historians claim, a Japanese blunder and that the subsequent state of American society was not, as often advertised, one of near perfect unity?

2. What cultural values separate the American and Japanese soldier? With what results?

3. What are the stages of the Soldier's Evolution? Of the Soldier's De-Evolution? Do you find reasonable each of these stages? And once the civilian-soldier-civilian conversion has been completed, what, if anything, remains?

4. Why does the American soldier become bitter? And if, as Jones asserts, the soldier's ultimate reaction to his experience is one of bitterness, why do Americans at large continue to regard so favorably the Second World War?

5. J. Glenn Gray, in his book <u>The Warriors</u>, develops the notion of "the enduring appeals of battle." Does James Jones grant their existence? Does he grant their centrality?

6. What are the author's attitudes towards women?

7. What are the various major strategic conceptions of the war that divide Allied leaders?

8. What, according to James Jones, are the war's principal effects at home?

9. Do you share James Jones' judgment regarding the Nuremberg and Tokyo war-crimes trials? Regarding the American use of the atomic bomb?

10. What is James Jones' objection to the way in which World War II is given its historical definition? To the way in which World War II is remembered today? What, to him, is the "truth," "the real story" of the war? Do you accept his contentions?

11. How would you summarize James Jones' definition of war's essential nature?

Questions Pertinent to Anthony B. Herbert's <u>Soldier</u>

1. Why does Anthony Herbert feel such intense love of the Army?

2. To what does Anthony Herbert attribute the Army's failure to win in
    Vietnam? What questions would you wish to pose to test his asser-
    tions? Does his analysis of Vietnam developments coincide with
    your own?

3. What are Anthony Herbert's qualifications for rendering such judg-
    ments? And would you pay more or less heed to his analysis of
    Vietnam than you would to Paul Baumer's explanation of why Germany
    lost World War One?

4. What are Anthony Herbert's attitudes toward

            the enemy;
            killing; and
            comradeship,

    and are they what we might have expected on the basis of previous
    readings?

Questions Pertinent to David Halberstam's The Best and the Brightest.

1. In the Author's Note (page 811), David Halberstam writes, "The question which intrigued me the most was why, why had it happened." What is the answer that his book proposes? Does the explanation for the Vietnam War rest in system (e.g. an Eastern Establishment National Security Elite), in process (e.g. the bureaucratic process), in ideology or in personality? Might different men have produced different policies?

2. Does David Halberstam propose a solution, changes that will ensure that Vietnam does not recur? If so, do they appear to you practicable?

3. The author asserts several times that those who establish American policy in Vietnam define it in ideological rather than national terms. To what ideology does he refer?

4. The book appears to create a composite Kennedy Man, a Walt McNamara Rostow-Bundy. What are his characteristics?

5. George Ball, although opposed to many aspects of the administration's Vietnam policy, decides to remain within government. How would you judge his decision?

6. Why is it that within the bureaucratic process deception becomes standard operating procedure?

7. Does David Halberstam's methodology—he says, for example, that regarding sources, you must trust him—undermine the book's authority?

Reduced Reading Assignment - Fawcett Crest Book edition

Chapter	1:	pages 9-17	Chapter 17:	pages 424-428, 431-439
	4:	pages 50-60, 76-81	18:	pages 440-449, 460-461
	5:	pages 82-108	19:	pages 488-521
	8:	pages 151-191	20:	pages 522-536
	9:	pages 192-193, 205-223	22:	pages 590-621
	10:	pages 224-227	23:	pages 622-650
	11:	pages 247-262	24:	pages 651-663, 679-682
	12:	pages 263-271, 291-295	25:	pages 683-713
	13:	pages 310-325	26:	pages 714-731
	14:	pages 326-333	27:	pages 732-741
	15:	pages 350-368	Epilogue:	pages 742-800
	16:	pages 369-376, 420-423	A Final Word:	pages 801-809

Questions Pertinent to Philip Caputo's <u>A Rumor of War</u>

1. What is the title of the book meant to express?

2. Can Philip Caputo be said to be one of the best and the brightest?

3. What impels Philip Caputo to join the United States Marine Corps?
   Is his motivation essentially idealistic or self-regarding? Are
   there in it echoes of others whose motives for seeking war we
   examined earlier?

4. Why, after such extensive training and indoctrination, does Philip
   Caputo find himself unprepared for Vietnam combat? Which elements
   of combat identified by J. Glenn Gray are here present? Absent?

5. In what ways does his conception of war alter as a result of his
   experience in Vietnam?

6. Who or what is responsible for the deaths of Le Du and Le Dung?

7. Philip Caputo reports that in battle he experienced the feeling of
   watching himself in a film (page 306). To what do you attribute
   this sense of himself as both participant and spectator?

8. Philip Caputo writes on page xii that "War is always attractive
   to young men who know nothing about it," but this is nonsense,
   for young men <u>always</u> know something of war. Please evaluate this
   counter-contention.

9. Which soldier is the more lost, Philip Caputo or Paul Baumer?

History A02, Sec. 25   War and Social Change in Twentieth-Century
                         America

Instructor: George H. Roeder, Jr.
Office: 12-D Harris Hall, phone 492-7261
Office Hours: 1:00-2:50, W; 11:00-11:50 F; by appointment
Home phone: 864-3351

Class Schedule: We will meet from 3 to 5 on Wednesday afternoon in Rm. 3370
at the main library. After an introductory session we will devote three ·
sessions each to World War I, World War II, and Vietnam. We will discuss
student papers in our final session on December 5.

NOTE: We have a regularly scheduled session on Wednesday, Nov. 21, the
day before Thanksgiving.

Required Readings:
William M. Tuttle, Race Riot: Chicago in the Red Summer of 1919 (by Oct. 3)
John M. Cooper, Jr., ed., Causes and Consequences of World War I (by Oct.17)
Richard Polenberg, War and Society: The United States, 1941-1945 (by Oct.31)

and one of the following (by Nov. 21):

Lawrence M. Baskir and William A. Strauss, Chance and Circumstance: The Draft
   The War, and the Vietnam Generation
C.D.B. Bryan, Friendly Fire
Alexander Kendrick, The Wound Within: America in the Vietnam Years, 1945-1974

Grading:
Class participation (25% of grade)
Two three to five page glorified book reports (30% of grade)
Research paper of ten or more pages in length (45% of grade)

The first report is due on October 17, the second on November 14, and the
research paper is due on December 5.

Class participation: Roughly 25% of your grade will be based on your
contributions to class discussions. I expect you to be thoroughtly
familiar with assigned readings, to give evidence that you have thought
carefully about this material, and to share with the class the results of
your independent reading and research. If you miss more than one session
during the quarter let me know the reason for your absence.

Glorified book reports: Write two three to five page papers, one on one
of the six books listed above under required readings and one on a book
chosen from the list of additional readings given below. After obtain-
ing my approval, you may substitute an appropriate book of your own
choice for one of the books from the list of additional readings. These
two papers count for 30% of your grade. You may hand in either one on
October, 17, and the other on November 14. In both papers answer the
following questions:

   1. In the author's view, did the war under discussion lead to
   social changes which probably would not have occurred, or would
   not have occurred at the same rate, or with quite the same consequences, had there been no war?

2. What is the nature of the evidence and reasoning which the author uses, implicitly or explicitly, to support this viewpoint?

3. Do you find this evidence and reasoning convincing? What further evidence, or what different use of available evidence, would help the author explain more clearly the relation between the war and the social changes under discussion?

You do not have to organize your paper around these questions, but somewhere in both reports you must deal with the issues they raise.

I define social change broadly to include changes in the distribution of wealth and power, the strength and direction of movements seeking reform of existing institutions or more radical changes, the status of groups such as blacks and women and the relations between these groups and other groups, the effectiveness and goals of labor organizations, the development and spread of new technologies, offical and popular attitudes toward civil liberties and toward the environment, and in prevailing moral, aesthetic, and intellectual codes or assumptions. I also include changes in the role of the United States in encouraging or resisting social change in other countries. In your reports I do not want you to describe all of the connections between war and social change mentioned in your book, but only those which seem most pertinent to an understanding of the issues discussed in the paper.

Research paper: Write a paper of ten pages or more in length in which you become the historian and confront the problem of describing the impact of war on twentieth-century American society. In the paper compare the impact of one war on at least two aspects of American life. For instance, you might compare the impact of World War I to that of World War II on Evanston's black community, or you might compare the impact which World War I had on Evanston blacks to the impact which it had on women in the community. Base the paper on assigned and recommended readings, on class discussions, and on independent research in some of the following sources: oral history interviews, and materials from the period under study, including newspapers, letters, magazines, government documents, trade journals, works of fiction, archival or manuscript collections, photographs, and artifacts.

I encourage you to discuss your research project with other students, but the organization and wording of the paper must be your own. Mention in the footnotes at appropriate points any source which you draw on heavily or which you quote or paraphrase. Use common sense in preparing your footnotes. They serve their purpose if they enable the reader to locate easily the source of a particular quotation, paraphrase, or concept.

Write a paper which does not deserve any of the following comments: "you rely too heavily on one or two sources in which the author has already organized the material for you", "you do nothing to place your topic in its historical context, or to show how it relates to themes developed in this course", "unclear writing and poor organization obscure the points which you are trying to make", "this is not a comparative paper--it is merely a paper on two different topics", "the paper lacks fresh insights because you have been content with stating the obvious", "you should reread every sentence in this paper and ask yourself, 'do I really believe that?'".

The research paper is due at the time of our final session on December 5 and will count for 45% of your grade.

Additional readings (these books are on reserve at the library):
Blum, John Morton, V Was for Victory
Bourne, Randolph, War and the Intellectuals: Collected Essays, 1915-1919
Dubofsky, Melvyn, We Shall be All: A History of the Industrial Workers of the World
Gruber, Carol S., Mars and Minerva: World War I and the Uses of Higher Learning in America
Halberstam, David, The Best and the Brightest
Levin, Jr., N. Gordon, Woodrow Wilson and World Politics
May, Henry F., End of American Innocence: A Study of the First Years of Our Own Time, 1912-1917
Perrett, Geoffrey, Days of Sadness, Years of Triumph: The American People, 1939-1945
Preston, Jr., William, Aliens and Dissenters: Federal Suppression of Radicals, 1903-1933
Rabe, David, Sticks and Stones
Trask, David F., ed., World War I at Home: Readings on American Life, 1914-1920

If you want to do further reading on your topic, a good place to start the search for appropriate books and articles would be in the bibliographies provided by Cooper, Polenberg, and Kendrick (see list of required readings). A particularly useful bibliography on the domestic impact of World War I is included in Ronald Schaffer, The United States in World War I: A Selected Bibliography, which is available in the reference room of the main library.

CITY UNIVERSITY OF NEW YORK, GRADUATE CENTER

Michael Wreszin   CUNY HISTORY U 757   Fall, 1976
                    WAR AND LIBERALISM IN 20TH CENTURY AMERICA

"Nothing I have found in my own reserach would support the conclusion that
the New Dealers conspired to involve the nation in war, and very little
would suggest an inevitable marriage of New Deal reform with war. Yet the
relationship between progressivism and war in the twentieth century State,
it should be added, is a subject which is imperfectly understood and one
which deserves more exploration." (Wm. E. Leuchtenburg, "The New Deal and
the Analogue of War," from Change and Continuity in 20th Century America,
eds., J. Braeman, R.H. Bremmer & E. Walters, 1964, p. 139 f/n # 181.)

This colloquium will pursue the question raised by Leuchtenburg in the statement
above. It is concerned with the relationship, if any, between 20th century
American reform and the mobilization for war. Is there any kind of symbiotic
relationship between war and the goals and objectives of modern reform?

REQUIRED READING FOR CLASS DISCUSSION:

1.   Arthur Ekirch, THE DECLINE OF AMERICAN LIBERALISM, Atheneum
2.   Herbert Croly, THE PROMISE OF AMERICAN LIFE, Dutton
3.   Walter Lippmann, DRIPT AND MASTERY: An Attempt to Diagnose the Current
     Unrest, Prentice Hall
4.   Christopher Lasch, THE NEW RADICALISM IN AMERICA: THE INTELLECTUAL AS A
     SOCIAL TYPE, Vintage
5.   Ronald Radosh & Murray N. Rothbard, A NEW HISTORY OF LEVIATHAN: ESSAYS ON
     THE RISE OF THE AMERICAN CORPORATE STATE, Dutton
6.   Ronald Radosh, PROPHETS ON THE RIGHT: PROFILES OF CONSERVATIVE CRITICS OF
     AMERICAN GLOBALISM, Simon & Schuster
7.   Carl Resek ed., RANDOLPH BOURNE: WAR AND THE INTELLECTUALS, Harper
8.   Reinhold Niebuhr, CHILDREN OF DARKNESS AND THE CHILDREN OF LIGHT, Scribners
9.   _____, MORAL MAN & IMMORAL SOCIETY, Scribners
10. Henry Fairlie, THE KENNEDY PROMISE, Dell
11. Richard Walton, COLD WAR AND COUNTER-REVOLUTION: THE FOREIGN POLICY OF JFK,
     Pelican
12. Richard Barnet, ROOTS OF WAR: THE MEN AND INSTITUTIONS BEHIND U.S. FOREIGN
     POLICY, Pelican
13. "The American Commonwealth," THE PUBLIC INTEREST, 10TH ANNIVERSARY ISSUE,
     Fall, 1975.
14. "America Now: A Failure of Nerve?" COMMENTARY, July 1975. (A Symposium)

XEROXED ARTICLES HOPEFULLY ON RESERVE IN LIBRARY AND INCLUDED IN REQUIRED READING

1.   Sidney Kaplan, "Social Engineers as Saviors: Effects of WWI on Some American
     Liberals," Jl OF THE HISTORY OF IDEAS
2.   Christopher Lasch, "The Making of the War Class," Columbia FORUM, Winter 1971.
3.   William Leuchtenburg, "Progressivism and Imperialism," MISSISSIPPI VALLEY
     HISTORICAL REVIEW, Vol. 39, Dec. 1952.
4.   William A. Williams, "Loans, Submarines & the Urge to Reform," in his
     anthology, THE SHAPING OF AMERICAN DIPLOMACY, pp. 547-597. Note particularly
     the Birdsall article.
5.   Barnard Baruch, "American Industry in the War: A Report of the War Industries
     Board," in Carroll W. Pursell Jr., ed., THE MILITARY-INDUSTRIAL COMPLEX.

6. J.P. Diggins, "Flirtation with Fascism: America's Pragmatic Liberals and Mussolini's Italy, AMERICAN HISTORICAL REVIEW, Jan. 1966.
7. W.A. Williams, "The Legend of Isolationism," in his THE TRAGEDY OF AMERICAN DIPLOMACY, chapter 4.
8. John D. Hicks, "The Diplomacy of Isolation," in his THE REPUBLICAN ASCENDENCY
9. Wm. E. Leuchtenburg, "The New Deal & the Analogue of War," in J. Braeman, R. Bremmer, E. Walters, eds., CHANGE AND CONTINUITY IN 20TH CENTURY AMERICA.
10. Paul Koistinen, "The Industrial-Military Complex in Historical Persective," BUSINESS HISTORY REVIEW, Winter 1967, also in C.W. Pursell, THE MILITARY INDUSTRIAL COMPLEX.
11. F.W. Fulbright, "In Thrall to Fear," THE NEW YORKER, Jan. 8, 1972. Appears also in his THE CRIPPLED GIANT and in ANNUAL READINGS IN AMERICAN HISTORY, Vol. II.
12. Hans J. Morganthau, "What Ails America," THE NEW REPUBLIC, Vol. 157, Oct. 28, 1967.
13. A. Schlesinger, Jr., "Presidential War," NYT MAGAZINE, Jan. 7, 1973

Books on Reserve in the Library

1. Daniel Bell, THE END OF IDEOLOGY: THE EXHAUSTION OF POLITICAL IDEAS IN THE FIFTIES
2. Charles Beard, THE DEVIL THEORY OF WAR
3. _____, PRESIDENT ROOSEVELT & THE COMING OF THE WAR
4. Richard Barnet , INTERVENTION & REVOLUTION
5. Mark Chadwin, THE HAWKS OF WORLD WAR II
6. Lawrence Dennis, IS CAPITALISM DOOMED
7. Charles Budd Forcey, THE CROSSROADS OF LIBERALISM
8. James Gilbert, DESIGNING THE INDUSTRIAL STATE: 1880-1940
9. Ellis Hawley, THE NEW DEAL AND THE PROBLEM OF MONOPOLY
10. Richard Hofstadter, ANTI-INTELLECTUALISM IN AMERICAL LIFE
11. R. Allan Lawson, THE FAILURE OF INDEPENDENT LIBERALISM
12. S. Martin Lipset ., POLITICAL MAN: THE SOCIAL BASIS OF POLITICS
13. Richard Pells, RADICAL VISIONS & AMERICAN DREAMS
14. A. Schlesinger, Jr., BITTER HEARITAGE
15. Frank Warren, LIBERALISM & COMMUNISM: THE RED DECADE REVISITED
16. Ronald Radosh, PROPHETS ON THE RIGHT

COURSE REQUIREMENTS: Students are responsible for having read the major reading assignment for each session of the colloquium and should come well prepared to engage in the discussion. There will be a writing assignment to be determined by the class. There will probably be a final exam during the week of January 10.

COURSE SCHEDULE OF READING AND DISCUSSION: Since this is to be a colloquium it will be run by all of us as a discussion seminar. Each week there is a general topic with a major reading assignment and some supplementary material. Tentatively the instructor will serve as the discussion leader, but he is not to monopolize the session and students should see that that doesn't happen. He will be permitted to make some opening remarks if he feels they are appropriate and helpful in starting the discussion. But all members of the colloquium should be PREPARED TO PARTICIPATE on the basis of their reading of the specific material and other knowledge they will bring to the discussion.

Week 1: Sept. 22: INTRODUCTION TO THE COURSE: Explanation and apology for missing the first scheduled session. Presentation of course purpose, reading list, requirements, possible changes, different selections on advise of students and discussion

of requirements, papers, exams, etc. And maybe some
introductory statement by the instructor - but only if
necessary.

Week 2: Sept. 29: DEFINITION OF POLITICAL TERMS

Basic Reading: Ekirch, THE DECLINE OF AMERICAN LIBERALISM, Preface,
Forward & 1st ten chapters, pp. 1-170
THE PUBLIC INTEREST, particularly the essays by Diamond,
Kristol, Huntington, Moynihan, Lipsett and Bell
Suggested supplementary Reading: Louis Hartz, THE LIBERAL TRADITION IN
AMERICA
Lionell Trilling, THE LIBERAL IMAGINATION
John Chamberlain, FAREWELL TO REFORM
R. Wiebe, THE SEARCH FOR ORDER

This session will be devoted to a discussion of political terminology -
liberal, conservative, radical, ideology, concensus - as they relate to
American political and social history in the 19th and 20th centuries.
What is the basic distinction between 19th and 20th century liberalism?
What accounts for its demise - if that is the case? How have these terms
changed in Post War II period? Are freedom and democracy compatible?

Week 3: Oct. 6: THE NEW PROGRESSIVE VISION

Basis Reading: Herbert Croly, THE PROMISE OF AMERICAN LIFE
Ekirch, DECLINE OF LIBERALISM, Chapter 11
Supplementary Reading: Forcey, Crossroads of Liberalism, ch. 1
A. Schlesinger, Jr., Intro. to Harvard Library, ed. of PROMISE

This session deals with the nationalist progressive classic. It is a long
and sometimes tedious work but it reflects the real thrust of the 20th
century reform movement. You will have to skim and gut the book but you
should read carefully his assault on Jeffersonian democracy, his apprecia-
tion of Hamilton, his position on militarism and foreign policy and his
attitudes toward elitism, liberty and democracy. How relevant are Croly's
ideas and how enduring his influence?

Week 4: Oct. 13: ESCAPE FROM THE NEW FREEDOM: MASTERY & SOCIAL CONTROL

Basic Reading: Walter Lippmann, DRIFT AND MASTERY
C. Lasch, NEW RADICALISM, Intro and chs. 1-5 with special
emphasis on ch. 5, "The Politics of Social Control"
Supplementary Reading: Forcey, Crossroads, ch. 3, "Walter Lippmann:
Voluntarist Liberal, 1909-1913
David Noble, THE PARADOX OF PROGRESSIVE THOUGHT
Morton White, SOCIAL THOUGHT IN AMERICA: THE REVOLT AGAINST
FORMALISM
E.A. Ross, SOCIAL CONTROL
R. Hofstadter, "The Rise of the Expert," and "Education in a
Democracy," both chapters of his ANTI-INTELLECTUALISM IN
AMERICAN LIFE
Charles Van Hise, CONCENTRATION & CONTROL
Ernest Poole, THE HARBOR (a novel)

This session is concerned with the concept of social control, elite management,
and social manipulation along with a suspicion of democracy as an ingredient of

American reform during the progressive period. What is the purpose of reform with respect to the existing locus of power? What is the reformers greatest fear? Who does the reformer see as his greatest opponent?

Week 5: Oct. 20: THE NEW CORPORATE LIBERALISM

Basic Reading: Radosh and Rothbard, eds., HISTORY OF NEW LEVIATHAN - The
Williams Intro.
David Eakins, "Policy Planning for the Establishment"
Martin Sklar, "Woodrow Wilson & the Political Economy of Modern
U.S. Liberalism" (all in R. & R. Leviathan)
Highly Recommended Supplementary Reading: James Weinstein, THE CORPORATE
IDEAL IN THE LIBERAL STATE
Gabriel Kolko, THE TRIUMPH OF CONSERVATISM: A REINTERPRETATION
OF AMERICAN HISTORY, 1900-1916

This session deals with the enlightened liberal business and industrial leadership which repudiates "laissez-faire" finds and ally in the State and adopts the principles of social control and social engineering in the interest of order and stability.

Week 6: Oct. 27: THE LIBERAL CORPORATE MANAGERS & THE WAR

Basic Reading: Murray N. Rothbard, "War Collectivism in World War I," in
R. & R., NEW HISTORY OF LEVIATHAN
Ekirch, ch. 12, "America Enters the Struggle for Power"
W.A. Williams, "Loans, Subs & the Urge to Reform" with special
emphasis on the Paul Birdsall article, "Neutrality and Economic
Pressures, 1914-1917," pp. 560-568. Read Docs carefully.
B. Baruch, "American Industry in the War"
C. Lasch, "The Making of the War Class"
Supplementary Reading: James Weinstein, "War as Fulfillment," ch. 8 of
Corporate Ideal

This session deals with the causes of American intervention, the degree to which war mobilization served corporate interests and was used as a model for the future organization of society.

Week 7: Nov. 3: THE MOTHLIKE GYRATION, PRAGMATIC ACQUIESCENCE: SNIFFING AT
THE HEMS OF POWER

Basic Reading: Resek, ed., BOURNE: WAR & THE INTELLECTUALS, Part I, "The
War" and selections 10, 12, 14
Lasch, "The New Republic & the War," ch. 6 of THE NEW RADICALISM
Sidney Kaplan, "Social Engineers as Saviors"
Wm. Leuchtenburg, "Progressivism & Imperialism"
Supplementary Reading: Forcey, Crossroads, Part III, Chs. 7 & 8. This is
a very relevant study of Croly, Lippmann and New Republic editors
role in the mobilization of thought for war - Lasch based much
of his comments on this work. Well worth reading in conjunction
with the basic reading.
Morton White, SOCIAL THOUGHT IN AMERICA *material on Dewey &
Bourne, particularly ch. 11, "Destructive Intelligence"
Carol S. Gruber, MARS AND MINERVA: WORLD WAR I & THE USES OF
THE HIGHER LEARNING IN AMERICA
Robert E. Osgood, IDEALS AND SELF INTEREST IN AMERICA'S FOREIGN
RELATIONS, particularly ch. 6 section 4 on New Republic
M. Wreszin, OSWALD GARRISON VILLARD: PACIFIST AT WAR, chs. 5 & 6

This session is concerned primarily with conflicting notions as to the role and responsibility of the intellectual in a democratic society. It centers on Bourne's classic critique of the new pragmatism. How does the intellectual influence the policy of the state? Can the intellectual serve the State and remain an intellectual?

Week 8: Nov. 10:   THE NEW ERA OF THE TWENTIES: REACTION OR CONTINUITY

Basic reading: M. Rothbard, "Herbert Hoover & the Myth of Laissez Faire,"
                     in THE NEW HISTORY OF LEVIATHAN
                J. Diggins, "Flirtation with Fascism: American Pragmatic Liberals
                     and Mussolini's Italy"
                W.A. Williams, "The Legend of Isolationism"
                Lasch, "The Education of Lincoln Steffens," ch. 8 of NEW RADICALISM
Suggested reading: Joan Hoff Wilson, AMERICAN BUSINESS AND FOREIGN POLICY
                     1920-1933
                Lincoln Steffens, AUTOBIOGRAPHY & Kaplans Biography of Steffens
                David A. Shannon, BETWEEN THE WARS: America 1919-1941, chs. 1-7

Was the decade of the Twenties a return to the age of McKinley? Or was it merely the continuation and culmination of ideas developed during the progressive era? What happened to the collaboration between corporate liberalism and liberal reformers?

Week 9: Nov. 17:   THE NEW DEAL & THE NEW WAR

Basic reading: Leuchtenburg, "The New Deal & the Analogue of War"
                Radosh, "The Myth of the New Deal," in NEW HISTORY OF LEVIATHAN
                Paul Koistinen, "The Industrial - Military Complex in Historical
                     Perspective
Supplementary reading: Elis Hawley, THE NEW DEAL AND THE PROBLEM OF MONOPOLY
                Richard Pells, RADICAL VISIONS AND AMERICAN DREAMS
                R.R. Allen Lawson, THE FAILURE OF INDEPENDENT LIBERALISM, 1930-1941
                Frank Warren, LIBERALS AND COMMUNISM: THE RED DECADE REVISITED
                _____, AN ALTERNATIVE VISION: THE SOCIALIST PARTY IN THE
                     1930s
                Barry Karl, ECONOMIC REORGANIZATION & REFORM IN THE NEW DEAL
                M. Wreszin, "The Dies Committee" in Schlesinger, Jr., and R. Bruns,
                     CONGRESS INVESTIGATES, 1792-1974

Emphasis of this section is on the alleged reform failures of the New Deal and the continued relationship and dependence of reform movements on mobilization for war to achieve reformist goals.

Week 10: Nov. 24:   WAR & THE INTELLECTUALS: ACT TWO

Basic reading: Ronald Radosh, PROPHETS ON THE RIGHT, chs. dealing with
                     the resistence to World War II. (That is the first chapter
                     of each profile.) I believe I failed to list this book
                     originally - but since it is so provocative it seems like a
                     good vehicle for discussion.
Supplementary reading: Charles Beard, THE DEVIL THEORY OF WAR
                Charles Beard, PRES. ROOSEVELT & THE COMING OF THE WAR
                Bruce Catton, "The WarLords in Washington," in Pursell, ed.,
                     THE MILITARY INDUSTRIAL COMPLEX

Richard Polenberg, WAR AND SOCIETY
Lawrence Dennis, IS CAPITALISM DOOMED

Discussion of how the liberal establishment narrows the limits of debate on a national question. Is it true that legitimate criticism was unfairly stifled?

Week 11: Dec. 1:   THE RETURN OF ORIGINAL SIN AS A POLITICAL DOCTRINE

Basic Reading: Reinhold Niebuhr, THE CHILDREN OF DARKNESS & THE CHILDREN
            OF LIGHT
            OR
            Neibuhr, MORAL MAN AND IMMORAL SOCIETY
            Lasch, "The Anti-Intellectualism of the Intellectuals" see
            specific critique of Niebuhr
Supplementary Readings: Richard Pells, RADICAL VISIONS AND AMERICAN DREAMS
            A. Schlesinger, Jr., "R. Niebuhr's Role in Americal Political
            Life & Thougth" in C. Kegley & R.W. Bretall, R. NIEBUHR: HIS
            RELIGIOUS, SOCIAL & POLITICAL THOUGHT
            M. Wreszin, "Taking Man's Measure" Essay review of Niebuhr's
            MAN'S NATURE AND HIS COMMUNITIES, The Nation, Jan. 3, 1966
            Donald Meyer, THE PROTESTANT SEARCH FOR POLITICAL REALITY

A discussion of Niebuhr as the intellectual and philosophical underpinning of post World War II school of political "realism" that has informed the architects of America's Foreign Policy and its limited expectations for more than piecemeal reform. An understanding of the thought and influence of Niebuhr is basic to an understanding of the nature of recent liberalism.

Week 12: Dec. 8:   PRAGMATISM VS. UTOPIA: THE VITAL CENTER

Basic Reading: A Schlesinger, Jr., THE VITAL CENTER
            W. Fulbright, "In Thrall to Fear"
            Lasch, last chapter of New Radicalism - comments on Schlesinger
Supplementary Reading: A. Schlesinger, Jr., THE POLITICS OF HOPE
            Jessie Lemisch, ON ACTIVE SERVICE IN WAR AND PEACE: POLITICS AND
            IDEOLOGY IN THE AMERICAN HISTORICAL PROFESSION
            Daniel Bell, THE END OF IDEOLOGY, ch. 6 and epilogue
            S.M. Lipsett, POLITICAL MAN, chs. 10, 13
            Noam Chomsky review of Schlesinger's BITTER HERITAGE in AMERICAN
            POWER AND THE NEW MANDARINS

A primer for Post-World War II liberalism and proper etiquette for budding Cold Warriors. Surely the most vigorous and articulate statement of the pragmatic liberal position in the years following the war.

Week 13: Dec. 15:   PRESIDENTIAL POWER AND NATIONAL SECURITY MANAGEMENT * WAR IS
            THE HEALTH OF THE STATE

Basic Reading: Ribhard Barnet, THE ROOTS OF WAR
            A. Schlesinger, Jr., "Presidential War" Students taking Prof.
            Schlesinger's current seminar may well wish to discuss his
            IMPERIAL PRESIDENCY
Supplementary Reading: Thomas Cronin, THE TEXTBOOK PRESIDENCY
            David Wise, THE POLITICS OF LYING

119

Essentially this session is concerned with the rise of the executive, the concentration of power, the development of the notion of national security perrogatives and the relationship of these developments to the reform mentality.

Week 14: Dec. 22: THE CRIPPLED CAMELOT

Basic Reading: Henry Fairlie, THE KENNEDY PROMISE
Richard Walton, COLD WAR AND COUNTER-REVOLUTION
Supplementary Reading: Schlesinger, Jr., Chapter on Kennedy in Imperial Presidency
Schlesinger, Jr., Appropriate Portions from 1000 Days
Richard Neustadt, PRESIDENTIAL POWER, afterward on JFK

History 170   Prof. John Kasson
TTh 9:30, Hamilton 425   Office Hrs: TTh 1:30-3:15
Fall 1982   Hamilton 473
                                                     Phone: 962-5004

TECHNOLOGY AND AMERICAN CULTURE

Schedule of Classes and Readings:

1. INTRODUCTION
    Aims and Expectations (Aug. 24)

2. THE EMERGENCE OF REPUBLICAN TECHNOLOGY
    Bases of American Technological Development (Aug. 26)
    The Notion of Republican Machine Technology (Aug. 31)
    The Beginnings of "the American System of Manufactures" (Sept. 2)

    Reading: John F. Kasson, Civilizing the Machine,* chapter 1
              Nathan Rosenberg, "Why in America?" in Otto Mayr and Robert C. Post, ed.,
                  Yankee Enterprise: The Rise of the American System of Manufactures
                  pp. 49-61
              Richard D. Brown, Modernization: The Transformation of American Life,
                  1600-1865, chapter 6

3. FACTORY TOWNS, WORKERS AND INDUSTRIAL DISCIPLINE IN ANTE-BELLUM AMERICA
    The Factory as Republican Community: Lowell, Massachusetts (Sept. 7)
    The Challenge to Lowell (Sept. 9)

    Reading: Kasson, Civilizing the Machine, chapter 2
             Excerpts from materials on Lowell

4. THE TECHNOLOGICAL SUBLIME
    The Rhetoric of Progressive Technology (Sept. 14)
    Machinery as Artistic Spectacle (Sept. 16)

    Reading: Kasson, Civilizing the Machine, chapters 3 and 4
              Excerpts from materials on the technological sublime

5. TENSIONS OF INDUSTRIAL DEVELOPMENT IN POST-BELLUM SOCIETY
    Inventors and Capitalists as Cultural Heroes (Sept. 21)
    The Dilemma of Industrial Workers (Sept. 23)

    Reading: Sigmund Diamond, ed., The Nation Transformed,* introduction, pp. 117-230
              Herbert G. Gutman, "Protestantism and the American Labor Movement," in
                  Work, Culture, and Society in Industrializing America, pp. 79-117
              Alfred D. Chandler, Jr., "The American System and Modern Management,"
                  in Mayr and Post, ed., Yankee Enterprise, pp. 153-170

6. TECHNOLOGY AND UTOPIA
    The Emergence of the Engineer (Sept. 28)
    Utopia and Dystopia (Sept. 30)

    Reading: Kasson, Civilizing the Machine, chapter 5
              Diamond, ed., The Nation Transformed, pp. 42-80

MIDTERM EXAMINATION (Oct. 5)

FALL BREAK (Oct. 7)

7. HENRY FORD AND THE IMPACT OF THE AUTOMOBILE
    The Adoption of the Automobile (Oct. 12)
    The Ambiguity of Henry Ford (Oct. 14)

    Reading: Keith Sward, The Legend of Henry Ford,* pp. 3-80, 161-288
             Robert Sklar, ed., The Plastic Age,* pp. 65-76

    Film: "A Car is Born" (Ford Motor Company)

8. TECHNOLOGY, THE ARTS AND MASS CULTURE IN THE 1920s
    A Hero for the Twenties: Charles Lindbergh (Oct. 19)
    The Artist in a Machine Age (Oct. 21)
    The Fruits of Technology (Oct. 26)
    An Advertising Ethic (Oct. 28)

    Reading: Sklar, ed., The Plastic Age, pp. 1-64, 77-118, 132-150, 251-306.
             Ruth Schwartz Cowan, "The 'Industrial Revolution' in the Home: Household
                Technology and Social Change in the 20th Century," Technology and
                Culture, 17 (Jan. 1976): 1-23
             John William Ward, "The Meaning of Lindbergh's Flight," American
                Quarterly, 10 (Spring 1958)

9. DEPRESSION DECADE: TECHNOLOGY IN CRISIS
    Technological Pastoralism (Nov. 2)
    The Planners' Visions (Nov. 4)
    Labor in the Thirties (Nov. 9)
    The "Machine Age" Ideal (Nov. 11)

    Reading: Warren Susman, ed., Culture and Commitment,* pp. 1-24, 45-56, 68-82,
             132-41, 187-92, 249-86, 296-326. Study photographs, pp. 329-369

    Films: "The City" (1939), directed by Pare Lorenz, text by Lewis Mumford, music
             by Aaron Copland. Shown at New York World's Fair, 1939.
           "Modern Times" (1936), directed by and starring Charles Chaplin.

10. WAR, TECHNOLOGICAL DEVELOPMENT, AND DEPERSONALIZATION
    Americans in World War Two: Assembly Lines and Front Lines (Nov. 16)
    From the Atomic Bomb to the Electronic Battlefield (Nov. 18)

    Reading: Robert Jay Lifton, History and Human Survival, pp. 117-155
             David H. Frisch, "Scientists and the Decision to Bomb Japan," in
                Robert S. Lewis, et al., Alamogordo Plus Twenty-Five Years, pp. 249-70
             Raphael Littauer and Norman Uphoff, ed., The Air War in Indochina,
                pp. 149-66

11. TECHNOLOGY AND CONTROL: PROSPECT AND RETROSPECT
    Technology and Environmental Concern (Nov. 23)
    The Perspective of Lewis Mumford (Nov. 30)
    Conclusion (Dec. 2)

    Reading: Donald Fleming, "Roots of the New Conservation Movement," Perspectives
                in American History, 6 (1972): 7-91
             Lewis Mumford, The Myth of the Machine: The Pentagon of Power,*
                pp. 164-320, 414-34

*Books marked with an asterisk have been ordered through Student Stores. Copies of
all readings are on reserve in the Undergraduate Library.

UNIVERSITY OF WISCONSIN

Department of History
Semester I, 1980-81
J.W. Dower
5114 Humanities (263-1972)

Office Hours: TT 12:30-2:00

HISTORY 573: PEARL HARBOR & HIROSHIMA

History 573 is an advanced undergraduate seminar that places emphasis
on student initiatives in research and class discussion. All participants
in the seminar this year will read a common selection of general
materials dealing with the events leading to Pearl Harbor, the conduct
of World War II in the Pacific, the dropping of the atomic bombs, and
Japan's surrender. Each student will also address a specific issue
or development in depth, and present this as both a class report and
final paper.

Individual topics ideally will break down so that roughly half of the
class deals with the road to Pearl Harbor, and half with the war
experience, the atomic bombs, or the final weeks of the war. The
individual topics may focus on events or interpretive controversies
(or, of course, both at once). They should be analytical and, to the
extent possible, based on "primary" materials (documents; contemporary
media accounts; autobiographies or other first-person accounts;
official publications; the original rather than summarized versions
of controversial arguments; etc.). Basic bibliographies are included
in some of the assigned readings, and will be supplemented by lists
of primary and secondary materials handed out in class.

Class reports should be one-half hour long, with an additional half
hour for discussion. There will be two reports each seminar, on
closely related topics. The two individuals giving reports are jointly
responsible for that day's seminar. Thus, they will also conduct
the discussions, and should get together beforehand to coordinate
their presentations. These reports will be discussed with the
instructor before they are presented.

The final paper is due December 9, and should be 20 - 30 typed, double-
spaced pages. It must include a bibliography and proper annotations
(footnotes can be given all in one place at the end), and reflect
attentiveness to basic editorial concerns. The paper should summarize
the problem addressed as accurately and succinctly (and eloquently!) as
possible, and convey the student's critical evaluation of the
issues involved.

The final grade will be based on the paper (2/3) plus class presentation
and contribution to class discussions (1/3).

READINGS

Assigned & Recommended for Purchase

Waller, George M., ed., Pearl Harbor: Roosevelt and the Coming
of the War, 3rd edition, Heath 1976.
Ienaga, Saburo, The Pacific War: World War II and the Japanese,
1931-1945, Pantheon 1978.
Havens, Thomas R.H., Valley of Darkness: The Japanese People and
World War II, Norton 1978.
Bernstein, Barton, ed., The Atomic Bomb: The Critical Issues
Little, Brown 1976.
Hersey, John, Hiroshima, Bantam 1946.

Assigned & Available as Class Handouts

Heinrichs, Waldo H., Jr., "1931-1937," in Ernest R. May & James C.
Thomson, Jr., ed., American-East Asian Relations: A Survey,
Harvard 1972.
Morton, Louis, "1937-1941," in Ernest R. May & James C. Thomson,
Jr., ed., American-East Asian Relations: A Survey, Harvard 1972.
Neumann, William L., "How American Policy Toward Japan Contributed
to War in the Pacific," in Harry Elmer Barnes, ed., Perpetual
War for Perpetual Peace: A Critical Examination of the Foreign
Policy of Franklin Delano Roosevelt and its Aftermath,
Caxton Printers 1953.
Chomsky, Noam, "The Revolutionary Pacifism of A.J. Muste: On the
Backgrounds of the Pacific War," in Chomsky, American Power
and the New Mandarins, Pantheon 1969.
United States Strategic Bombing Survey, Summary Report (Pacific
War), 32 pgs.
————————————————, Japan's Struggle to End the
War, pp. 1-22.
————————————————, The Effects of Atomic Bombs
on Hiroshima and Nagasaki, pp. 1-23.

Recommended

Morley, James W., ed., Dilemmas of Growth in Prewar Japan,
Princeton 1974.
————————, Japan's Foreign Policy: A Research Guide,
Columbia 1974.
Borg, Dorothy & Shumpei Okamoto, ed., Pearl Harbor as History:
Japanese-American Relations, 1931-1941, Columbia 1973.
Butow, Robert J.C., Japan's Decision to Surrender, Stanford 1954.
Baker, Paul R., ed., The Atomic Bomb: The Great Decision, 2nd
revised edition, Dryden Press 1976.
Fogelman, Edwin, ed., Hiroshima: The Decision to Use the A-Bomb,
Scribner 1964.

TENTATIVE CALENDAR

I. INTRODUCTORY SESSIONS

September 2   Course description, etc.

September 9   Tentative assignment of individual topics and back-
               ground lecture

September 16   Movie (Japan: A Century of Imperialism) and discussion

September 23   Background lecture and discussion

II. THE ROAD TO PEARL HARBOR

September 30

October 7

October 14   Movie (Know Your Enemy: Japan)

October 21

October 28

III. THE WAR & THE ATOMIC BOMBS

November 4

November 11

November 18

November 25   Movie (Hiroshima, Nagasaki)

December 2

December 9   Papers due

SUGGESTED INDIVIDUAL TOPICS

The Road to Pearl Harbor

The official US version [as seen in Foreign Relations of the United States, the congressional Pearl Harbor Hearings, etc.]

The official US version as seen in memoirs and the like [Hull, Grew, Stimson, Byrnes, Truman, etc.]

The Hull-Nomura talks of 1945 as seen from both sides [FRUS, Hull, Ike's translation of minutes of top-level Japanese meetings etc.]

Japanese strategic planning culminating in Pearl Harbor [Ike, various writings by Crowley, official US studies, etc.]

"Japan's case" as seen in writings at the time as well as translated memoirs by Japanese participants.

The US media and events leading to Pearl Harbor [analysis of such journalistic vehicles as The New York Times, Time, Life, Newsweek, a local newspaper, etc.]

The impending crisis as portrayed in the Japanese media available in English [Contemporary Japan, Trans-Pacific, The Nippon Times, etc.]

The impending crisis as depicted in cartoons, movies, etc.

The debate over why the US was caught by surprise at Pearl Harbor [Wohlstetter, congressional hearings, etc.]

The "Back Door to War"-debate among US academics [Beard, Barnes, Tansil, Newman]

The Magic intercepts of Japan's secret messages [available on microfilm]

Leftist analyses of the crisis of the 1930s (Amerasia, Far Eastern Survey, Trotzky, Stalin, Comintern, etc.]

IPR (Institute of Pacific Relations) conference reports and publications on "Problems of the Far East" prior to 1941.

The scholarly debate over Japanese "Fascism" [Maruyama, Halliday, Tanin and Yohan, Hobsbawn, Duus and Okamoto, Fletcher, Berger, etc.]

The debate over the role of the emperor [Bergamini, Sheldon, Harada-Saionji diary, Kido diary, Titus, etc.]

SUGGESTED INDIVIDUAL TOPICS

The War & the Atomic Bombs

Summary of Japanese strategic policy

Summary of US strategic policy

The war as portrayed in US media [photographs, articles, racial interpretations of Japanese behavior, etc.]

War movies

Wartime literature [Japanese in translation, as well as Western]

The debate over Japanese war guilt [Minear, IMTFE Judgment, dissent of Justice Pal, etc.]

Effects of strategic bombing on Japan [based on the USSBS reports]

The development of the A-bomb

The decision to drop the A-bombs [the options, controversions etc.]

Japanese accounts of the A-bomb experience

The Soviet entry into the war in August 1945 [the Yalta debate, etc.]

Japan's decision to surrender

University of Virginia

HIST 101C   INTRODUCTORY SEMINAR   James C. Baxter
Spring 1981   The Atomic Bombings of   Rouss 209
                     Hiroshima and Nagasaki   924-7972

Description of the course
      The atomic bomb changed warfare, and it changed the world.
America's use of its new weapon in August 1945 may have helped to
hasten the conclusion of World War II: unquestionably it caused
great loss of life and human suffering. To posterity, the dropping
of the bombs bequeathed dimensions of instantaneous and lingering
destruction that few could even have imagined before that fateful
month. President Truman and his successors and authorities in other
nations that have developed nuclear arms have made strategic decisions
with moral implications unlike those of statesmen and military leaders
of earlier ages. The consequences of those decisions affect us all.
      This seminar considers the development of the A-bomb, the
controversial decision to drop the two bombs, the impact of the bombs
on Japan's decision to surrender, the use of the bombs and the beginnings of the Cold War, the effects of the bombs on the Japanese,
strategic and moral aspects of the bomb, and the influence of the
bomb on the postwar world and postwar Japanese society.
      Readings will be selected from primary sources--papers, diaries
and memoirs of statesmen, scientists, military leaders, and ordinary
folk--and secondary accounts, including historical fiction.

Books
      The following have been ordered at Newcomb Hall Bookstore:
Bernstein, Barton J., ed., The Atomic Bomb: The Critical Issues.
Feis, Herbert, The Atomic Bomb and the End of World War II.
Hachiya, Michihiko, Hiroshima Diary.
Ibuse, Masuji, Black Rain.
Lifton, Robert, Death in Life.

Essays
      Four papers of approximately three typewritten pages must
be submitted. Due dates are February 24, March 24, April 7, and
April 28. For topic assignments, see below.

Grading
      Each paper counts 20%. A grade for seminar discussion, worth
20%, will be given; the quality of your contribution, as well as the
frequency with which you participate, will be evaluated.

                    TOPICS AND ASSIGNMENTS

Jan. 27   Introduction

Feb. 3   (I) Reading History, (II) Historiography of the Bombs,
            (III) Technical Background
            Reading: See page 2

Norman Cantor and Richard Schneider, How to Study
   History, chapters 5 and 6.
Bernstein, The Atomic Bomb: The Critical Issues, pp. vii-xi
Isaac Asimov, The Intelligent Man's Guide to Science. I:
   The Physical Sciences, pp. 469-478.
Margaret Gowing and Lorna Arnold, The Atomic Bomb, pp. 30-43

Feb. 10   The Competition. . .
           (1) David Irving, The German Atomic Bomb, pp. 263-303.
           (2) J. W. Dower. "Science, Society, and the Japanese
               Atomic-Bomb Project During World War II." Bulletin
               of Concerned Asian Scholars, X, 2 (1978).
           (3) Deborah Shapley, "Nuclear Weapons History: Japan's
               Wartime Bomb Projects Revealed," and response by
               Charles Weiner, Science, 199 (1978), pp. 152-157, 728.
           (4) A. Kramish, Atomic Energy in the Soviet Union (skim).

           . . . and the Manhattan Project
           (5) Leslie R. Groves, Now It Can Be Told (read in the
               manner recommended by Cantor and Schneider).

Feb. 17   The "Orthodox" View of the Justifiability of Dropping the
              Bombs
           Herbert Feis, The Atomic Bomb and the End of World War II.

Feb. 24   Revisionist Views of the Dropping of the Bombs. . .
           Working with two other students, read and prepare to dis-
           cuss (1), (2),   (3), or (4).
           (1) Gar Alperovitz, Atomic Diplomacy, pp. 55-63, 91-126,
               176-200, 226-242.
               _____. Cold War Essays. pp. 51-73.
               Bernstein, comments on Feis, comments on Alperovitz,
               The Atomic Bomb: The Critical Issues.
           (2) Martin J. Sherwin, A World Destroyed: The Atomic
               Bomb and the Grand Alliance.
               Bernstein comments (see (1) above).
           (3) Bernstein, "Roosevelt, Truman, and the Atomic Bomb,
               1941-1945," Political Science Quarterly, 90 (1975), 23-6
               _____, "Perils and Politics of Surrender: Ending
               the War with Japan and Avoiding the Third Atomic Bomb."
               Pacific Historical Review, 46 (1977), 1-27.
               _____. "Quest for Security: American Foreign
               Policy and International Control of Atomic Energy,
               1942-1946," Journal of American History, 60 (1974),
               1003-1044.
               _____, "The Uneasy Alliance: Roosevelt, Churchill,
               and the Atomic Bomb, 1940-1945," Western Political
               Quarterly, 29 (1976), 202-230.
               _____. comments (see (1) above).

Feb. 24   . . . and a Post-Revisionist View
  (cont.)   (4) John L. Gaddis. The United States and the Origins
                 of the Cold War. 1941-1947.
                 Bernstein comments, The Atomic Bomb: The Critical Issue

Feb. 24   ESSAY DUE. Compare and contrast Feis and the writer whom
             you considered for the seminar meeting of Feb. 24.

Mar. 3   History and Literature: Hiroshima
             Masuji Ibuse. Black Rain.

Mar. 10   Experiences of the Victims: Hiroshima
             (1) Michihiko Hachiya, Hiroshima Diary.
             (2) Japan National Preparatory Committee. A Call from
                 Hibakusha of Hiroshima and Nagasaki.

Mar. 24   Nagasaki
             (1) Groves, Now It Can Be Told, pp. 341-355.
             (2) Kyōko Hayashi, "Ritual of Death," Japan Interpreter,
                 XII, 1 (1978). (Xerox file.)
             (3) Takashi Nagai, We of Nagasaki.
             (4) A Call from Hibakusha of Hiroshima and Nagasaki (see
                 March 10).

Mar. 24   ESSAY DUE. Write an essay evaluating one or more of the
             works that you read for the meetings of March 3, 10. and 24

Mar. 31   Did the Bombs Hasten the Ending of the War?
             (1) Joseph Alsop and David Joravsky, "Was the Hiroshima
                 Bomb Necessary? An Exchange," New York Review of
                 Books, XXVII, 16 (Oct. 23,1980).
             (2) With two other students, read and prepare to discuss
                 one of the following:
                 (a) R. J. C. Butow. Japan's Decision to Surrender.
                 (b) The Pacific War Research Society, Japan's
                      Longest Day.
                 (c) John Toland, The Rising Sun.
                 (d) Lester Brooks. Behind Japan's Surrender.

Apr. 7   Were the Bombs Necessary?
             (1) Bernstein, The Atomic Bomb, pp. 29-56.
             (2) Joseph L. Marx, Nagasaki: The Necessary Bomb, pp. 198-2
             (3) W. F. Craven and J. L. Cate, eds., The Army Air Forces
                 in World War II, V: The Pacific: Matterhorn to Naga-
                 saki. pp. 726-756.
             (4) Sherwin (see Feb. 24) chapter 8.
             (5) Kenneth M. Glazier, "The Decision to Use Atomic
                 Weapons Against Hiroshima and Nagasaki," Public Policy,
                 XVIII (1969) 463-516.

             (6) Bernstein, "Doomsday II," New York Times Magazine,
                 July 27, 1975.   129

Apr. 7   (7) Morton Grodzins and Eugene Rabinowitch, eds., <u>Atomic</u>
(cont.)   <u>Age: Forty-Five Scientists and Scholars Speak</u>.

Apr. 7   ESSAY DUE. Write an essay evaluating the argument over whet
            the dropping of the atomic bombs was necessary to bring the
            war to a conclusion.

Apr. 14   American Leaders and the Atomic Bomb
            (1) Working with another student, select a biography, a
                book of memoirs, a diary, or a collection of letters
                or papers of an American who was involved in the
                decisions to develop and use the atomic bomb. Prepare
                to give a critical introduction of the work to the
                class, and to discuss the role played by the person
                whose work you have looked at.
            (2) Working with another student. look at the transcript
                of the interview with Norman Ramsey. Kenneth Bainbridge,
                Charles Corvell. or Harvey Bundy in the Columbia
                University Oral History Collection (on microfiche,
                available in the Periodical Room of Alderman Library).
                Evaluate the transcript as a source of evidence for
                a historian of the development of the atomic bomb.
            (3) Locate the papers of Edward Stettinius. Do they
                contain anything of value to a student of the atomic
                bomb, its development. or the decision to use it?

Apr. 21   The Effects of the Bombs on the Japanese
            (1) Working with two other students, read Robert Lifton,
                <u>Death in Life</u>.
            (2) John E. Endicott, <u>Japan's Nuclear Option</u>, pp. 91-101.
            (3) Hirosharu Seki. "Nuclear Proliferation and Our Option,"
                <u>Japan Quarterly</u>, 22 (Jan./Mar. 1975). 13-21.

Apr. 28   Americans' Feelings About the Bomb
            (1) Michael Yavenditti,"The American People and the Use
                of Atomic Bombs on Japan: 1940s," <u>The Historian</u>,
                XXXVI (Feb. 1974). (Xerox file.)
            (2) Sheila K. Johnson, <u>American Attitudes Toward Japan,</u>
                <u>1941-1975</u>, pp. 33-45.
            (3) Dwight Macdonald in Bernstein, <u>The Atomic Bomb</u>, pp. 142
            (4) Consult one of the indexes. abstracts, or current
                bibliographies listed in the guide "American History:
                Selected Reference Sources in Alderman Library."
                Select an article or essay on atomic weapons policy
                or the dilemmas of existence in a world with atomic
                weapons. Limit your choice to articles or essays that
                have relevance today. Locate and read the article or
                essay.

Apr. 28   ESSAY DUE. Write a critique of the book that you examined
           for the seminar meeting of April 14.

May 5   Opinions
           Meet at 148 Mimosa Drive at 5 p.m.
           Consult the Public Affairs Information Service Annual
           Cumulated Bulletin (Ref. Z71°3.P9) and find out what
           was published about atomic weapons during the past decade.

History 134 E
Professor Keith Nelson

Autumn, 1980
M-W-F, 10 a.m.

IMPERIALISM IN AMERICAN HISTORY

Course Description

The course is concerned with whether or not (and to what extent) the United States has been or is an imperialistic nation in its relations with other countries and peoples. In pursuing this question, the course focuses on the causes and effects of American behavior toward less powerful nations, from our early dealings with the Indians, Mexico, and Canada, to our twentieth century interventions and involvements in Latin America, Europe, Africa, and Asia. We shall examine radical, liberal, and conservative interpretations of such activity, including the theories of Hobson, Lenin, Schumpeter, Fieldhouse, Mao Tse-tung, and others.

Course Objectives

We have several objectives in this class:

1) to familiarize ourselves with the great ideological traditions (and to ascertain our own ideological preferences), particularly as they relate to and help to understand theories of imperialism;

2) to examine carefully the major theories of imperialism and to try to determine how they can be tested;

3) to look into the psychological and social dimensions of imperialism as well as the economic and political;

4) to place modern "imperialist" activity in its world-historical context;

5) to place American "imperialist" activity in its international context;

6) to identify the changes and continuities in relevant American behavior over the last 300 years;

7) to establish the connections between the activities of multi-national corporations and national behavior;

8) to determine what can be done to reduce and eliminate exploitative relationships between peoples.

Examinations, Papers, Discussion, and Grades

There will be one midterm, two short papers, and a final exam. The final course grade will be based 1/4 on the midterm, 1/4 on the papers, 1/4 on the final exam, and 1/4 on class discussion. Assignments have been designed so as to facilitate class discussion. Discussion questions will be distributed prior to each class meeting. This is primarily a discussion, not a lecture course, although a number of lectures will be given.

132

Books to Purchase

Robin W. Winks, ed., <u>British Imperialism: Gold, God, Glory</u>
(Holt, Rinehart, & Winston, 1963, $5.95)

Thomas G. Paterson, ed., <u>American Imperialism and Anti-Imperialism</u>
(Crowell, 1973, $4.50)

Felix Greene, <u>The Enemy: What Every American Should Know About Imperialism</u>
(Vintage, 1970, $2.45)

Charles P. Kindleberger, <u>America in the World Economy</u>
(Foreign Policy Association, 1977, $2.35)

Lloyd N. Cutler, <u>Global Interdependence and the Multinational Firm</u>
(Foreign Policy Association, 1978, $2.00)

Paul E. Sigmund, <u>The Overthrow of Allende</u>
(Pittsburgh, 1977, $5.95)

Books and Articles on Reserve (and Available for Purchase at Kinko's)

George Lichtheim, <u>Imperialism</u>
(Praeger, 1971)

Richard W. Van Alstyne, <u>The Rising American Empire</u>
(Quadrangle, 1965)

N. Gordon Levin, <u>Woodrow Wilson and World Politics: America's Response
to War and Revolution</u>
(Oxford, 1968)

Geoffrey Barraclough, "The Haves and the Have-Nots"
<u>The New York Review of Books</u>, (May 13, 1976), pp. 31-41.

"International Development", <u>Great Decisions '78</u>
(Foreign Policy Association, 1979), pp. 48-56.

Department of State, <u>Current Policy No. 136</u>, "Foreign Assistance Programs
for FY 1981", February, 1980.

Murray Seeger, "'American' Europe No Longer Threat", <u>LA Times</u>,
December 17, 1978.

"Global Companies: Too Big to Handle?", <u>Newsweek</u>, November 20, 1972,
pp. 96-104.

Robert L. Heilbroner, "None of Your Business", <u>The New York Review of Books</u>
(March 20, 1975), pp. 6-10.

Books and Articles on Reserve (Continued)

    Richard J. Barnet, _Intervention and Revolution_
        (World Publishing, 1968)

    William Taubman, ed., _Globalism and Its Critics: The American Foreign_
        Policy Debate of the 1960's
        (Heath, 1973)

    "The U. S. S. R.: A Fortress State in Transition", _Time_,
        June 23, 1980, pp. 22-29.

    Department of State , _Current Policy No. 99_, "Communism in Africa",
        October, 1979.

    William Sweet, "Soviet Adventurism", _New Republic_, December 8, 1979,
        pp. 21-23.

    Robert G. Neumann, "Afghanistan: In the Soviets' Imperialist Grasp",
        LA Times, January 6, 1980.

Schedule of Classes (the Assignment Must be Read by the Day of Class)

    Mon., Sept. 29 - - - Introduction and Orientation
    Wed., Oct. 1 - - - - Hobson and Lenin - - - -(Winks, 1-8, 11-25, 26-30)
    Fri., Oct. 3 - - - - Schumpeter - - - - - - -(Winks, 82-91)

    ———————

    Mon., Oct. 6 - - - - Fieldhouse - - - - - - -(Winks, 35-50)
    Wed., Oct. 8 - - - - The Imperialists - - - -(Winks, 56-61, 77-81)
                  (Lecture: The Relevance of Ideology)
    Fri., Oct. 10 - - - Ancient Imperialism - -(Lichtheim, 3-23)

    ———————

    Mon., Oct. 13 - - - Early Modern Imperialism - - -(Lichtheim, 24-60)
    Wed., Oct. 15 - - - Liberal Imperialism - - - -(Lichtheim, 61-97)
    Fri., Oct. 17 - - - The Conception of an American
                  Empire - - - - - - - - - - - -(Van Alstyne, 1-53)

    ———————

    Mon., Oct. 20 - - - Louisiana and the Monroe
                  Doctrine - - - - - - - - - -(Van Alstyne, 54-99)
    Wed., Oct. 22 - - - Manifest Destiny and
                  Continuing Expansion - - - -(Van Alstyne, 100-146)
                  FIRST ESSAY DUE

Fri., Oct. 24 - - - Spanish American War, Part 1: La Feber,
Leuchtenburg, and Hofstadter
- - - - - - - - - - - - -(Paterson, 1-33)

Mon., Oct. 27 - - - Spanish American War, Part II: Beale,
Grenville, Young, and Pratt
- - - - - - - - - - - - -(Paterson, 34-63)

Wed., Oct. 29 - - - Spanish American War, Part III:
McCormick, Williams, and May
- - - - - - - - - - - - -(Paterson, 64-91)

Fri., Oct. 31 - - - MIDTERM EXAM

Mon., Nov. 3 - - - - America and World War: 1917 - - -(Levin, 1-49)
(Lecture: America, Hartz, and Levin)

Wed., Nov. 5 - - - - America and Wilson's Peace: 1919
- - - - - - - - - - -(Levin, 123-125, 154-182)

Fri., Nov. 7 - - - - Neo-Imperialism - - - -(Greene, 69-110)

Mon., Nov. 10 - - - The Foreign Aid Fraud - -(Greene, 112-147)

Wed., Nov. 12 - - - Plunder and Satellization - - -(Greene, 148-215)

Fri., Nov. 14 - - - From Marx to Mao- - - - - -(Lichtheim, 134-169)

Mon., Nov. 17 - - - The Haves and Have-Nots - -(Barraclough, Great
Issues, '78)

Wed., Nov. 19 - - - American Trade Policy - - -(Kindleberger, 3-40)

Fri., Nov. 21 - - - American Aid - - (Kindleberger, 40-62; State
Department, #136)

Mon., Nov. 24 - - - American Investment - - -(Kindleberger, 63-90;
Seeger)
SECOND ESSAY DUE

Wed., Nov. 26 - - - American Globalism and Its Critics
- - -(Barnet, 225-254; Taubman, 3-9, 12-17,
55-66, 133-147)

Fri., Nov. 28 - - - THANKSGIVING HOLIDAY

Mon., Dec. 1 - - - - The Multinationals - -(Newsweek; Heilbroner;
Cutler, 3-50)

Wed., Dec. 3 - - - - Contemporary "Imperialism": Chile, 1973
- -(Sigmund, 92-125, 141-170, 188-201, 231-244)
Fri., Dec. 5 - - - - Contemporary "Imperialism": Afghanistan, 1980
- -(Time; State Dept., #99; Sweet; Neumann)

Thursday, December 11, 1980 - - - FINAL EXAM - - -(1:30 - 3:30 p.m.)

BROWN UNIVERSITY

History 198H   Graduate Course   Professor Neu
Spring Term, 1983

The American Experience in Vietnam

History and Diplomacy
Feb. 14

   George Herring, America's Longest War, all of this*

Feb. 21

   Leslie H. Gelb and Richard K. Betts, The Irony of Vietnam:
      The System Worked, parts 1, 4, and 5*

Feb. 28

   Frances Fitzgerald, Fire in the Lake, part 1 and chapters 13-17*

March 7

   Henry Kissinger, White House Years, chapters 8, 12, 23, 25, 27,
      31-34, and Years of Upheaval, chapters 2, 8, and 25

Ethical Choices and Domestic Conflicts
March 14

   Daniel Ellsberg, Papers on the War, introduction and pp. 234-309*
   Guenter Lewy, America in Vietnam, preface and chapters 6-10 and
      epilogue*

March 21

   Godfrey Hodgson, America in Our Time, chapters 1 and 13-25*

March 28

   Arthur M. Schlesinger, Jr., Robert Kennedy and His Times,
      chapters 19 and 30-41*

Past Mistakes and Future Policy
April 11

   Norman Podhoretz, Why We Were in Vietnam, all of this*

April 18

   Earl C. Ravenal, Never Again, all of this*

April 25

   Paper reports

May 2

   Paper Reports

137

May 16 PAPERS DUE (two copies)

*All of these books are in the bookstore. Most volumes are also on reserve, along with the <u>Senator Gravel Edition</u> of the Pentagon Papers.

Absence from seminars

Any student who misses a seminar meeting must write a book report on the assigned reading.

Late Papers and Incompletes

I will not give extensions beyond the May 16 deadline, or grant incompletes, unless a student is confronted with a serious personal or medical problem.

City University of New York, Graduate Center

M. Wreszin   History CP-10-2   Spring, 1982
Queens College
                           THE U.S. & THE VIETNAM WAR

A study of the United States intervention in Vietnam and the
impact of the war on Vietnam and on American life and culture.
The course will focus on the diplomatic, political, social &
cultural aspects of the war rather than on the military history.

The following syllabus, reading list and course schedule is
tentative and may be subject to change without notice.

REQUIRED READING: The following books have been ordered through the college
Book Store:

1. Francis Fitzgerald, FIRE IN THE LAKE: THE VIETNAMESE & THE AMERICANS IN
            VIETNAM   Vintage V-927

2. Gareth Porter, ed., VIETNAM: A HISTORY IN DOCUMENTS, NAL Meridian Book

3. Grahm Greene, THE QUIET AMERICAN, Penguin

4. Guenther, Lewy, AMERICA IN VIETNAM, Oxford Univ. Press

5. Todd Gitlin, THE WHOLE WORLD IS WATCHING: MASS MEDIA IN THE MAKING &
            UNMAKING OF THE NEW LEFT, Univ. of California Press

6. Gloria Emerson, WINNERS AND LOOSERS: Battles, Retreats, Gains, Losses
            and Ruins from a Long War, in paper, Harcourt Brace and J.
            Hardcover remainders, Random at Barns and Noble

7. There could be another book and there may be material on reserve.

THERE WILL BE A SUBSTANTIAL WRITING ASSIGNMENT. NO MIDTERM IS PLANNED. THERE
WILL BE A FINAL EXAM.

1. Feb. 3:   INTRODUCTION TO THE COURSE AND TO THE BIAS OF THE INSTRUCTOR:
               COURSE PERSPECTIVE, COMMENT ON THE NATURE OF THE HISTORICAL
               DISCIPLINE AND THE GENERAL REQUIREMENTS.

2. Feb. 10:   VIETNAM VIEWED WITHIN THE CONTEXT OF THE COMPLETION AND URGENCY
               OF ECONOMIC DEVELOPMENT AND POLITICAL MODERNIZATION; VIETNAM
               WITHIN THE CONTEXT OF 20TH CENTURY U.S. GLOBALISM; HISTORICAL
               PRECEDENT FOR VIETNAM - THE PHILIPPINES & WILSONIAN UNIVERSALISM;
               Beg. of French & U.S. collaborative intervention

               Francis Fitzgerald, FIRE IN THE LAKE, Preface and Part I, The
               Vietnamese pp. 3-96
               Gareth Porter, Docs, #'s 1, 4, 11, 26, 30, 31, 33,*37-38, 40
               41-42, 46, 48, 49, 50, 55, *57, *60 (I have made a note of
               these specific docs as I have perused them. You may find
               others of more significance. (*)Asterisked docs seemed to me

                                    139

to contain material of particular relevance to points made
in class discussion and lectures.

3. **Feb. 17:** THE FRENCH COLONIAL EXPERIENCE AND EARLY UNITED STATES INTEREST
IN VIETNAM; THE DIEM REGIME INTO CAMELOT; ANTI-COMMUNISM AS
FOUNDATION OF AMERICAN FOREIGN POLICY - in Europe, in Asia and
at Home

Fitzgerald, pp. 96-314 (This is for the following week also)
but note material on Diem vs. NLF and particularly the neat
portrait of the American vision pp. 307-314
Grahm Greene, THE QUIET AMERICAN
Guenther Lewy, AMERICA IN VIETNAM, Intro and up to p. 20
Class discussion this week or next on GREENE'S PORTRAIT AND
F.F.'S interpretation of the Vietnamese vision
Porter Docs #'s 63, 65, 66-67, 68, *69, 70 (Actually all of
these Docs up through 1954 deserve perusal to see American
dilemma. # 73, 75-6, 78, 80, 83, 85, 87, 91, 93, 98, 101,
103, 105, 106, 107, 110, 113, 116, 118, 120, 122, 123, 125,
126, 128

4. **Feb. 24:** THE KENNEDY YEARS: THE INTELLECTUAL'S PRIVATE WAR CONDUCTED
BY THE BEST AND THE BRIGHTEST

Fitzgerald, review pertinent material 163-314, 315-351
Guenther Lewy, AMERICA IN VIETNAM, pp. 20-36
Porter, Docs #'s 73, 76, 77 again peruse all these docs up to
63 - picking and choosing those that document your understanding
of American intervention

5. **Mar. 3 & Mar. 10:** FROM JFK TO LBJ: THE AMERICANIZATION OF VIETNAM AND OF
THE WAR

Fitzgerald, chs. 7-15, pp. 352-536 (184 fact-filled pages as
well as strong interpretation)
Lewy, pp. 30-127; His first 6 chapters deal with the fighting
of the war. Chs. 7-11 take up such issues as American
immorality, Atrocites, Media distortion, etc. So, actually,
those later chapters may well fit the Kennedy and Johnson
years. I suggest you use Lewy to contrast with Fitzgerald -
whom he challenges and repudiates. Read Lewy, ch. 11 on
decision to bomb north, pp. 374-404.
Porter, Docs #'s

6. **Mar. 17-24:** RESISTANCE: THE RISE OF AN ANTI-WAR MOVEMENT, A COUNTER-
CULTURE AND THE IMPACT OF AMERICAN SOCIETY, CULTURE AND POLITICAL
LIFE. THE INTRICATE ROLE OF THE MEDIA IN THE COLOR TV WARS AT
HOME AND ABROAD. THE WAR ON THE CAMPUS

Todd Gitlin, THE WHOLE WORLD IS WATCHING up to p. 180
Gloria Emerson, WINNERS AND LOOSERS. Begin reading this book
G. Lewy, begin reading Lewy chs. 7 (pp. 223) through ch. 9
(pp. 343)

7. Mar. 31:   NIXON: SECRET WAY TO END THE WAR: VIETNAMIZATION THROUGH AERIAL
              ESCALATION

              Fitzgerald, pp. 537-567
              Lewy, pp. 127-222, ch. 11 p. 404 on Bombing under Nixon
              Porter Docs #'s 237 ff.
              Gloria Emerson, continue reading her book

8. Apr. 14:   NIXON'S WAR CONTINUED -

              Film: HEARTS AND MINDS

              Gitlin, 180 to the end

              Discussion of Film, propaganda, media distortion

At this point there are only four meetings of the class left. I am now working
on scheduling some visitors, veterans of Vietnam War and perhaps some veterans
of the War at Home and hopefully some other films.

UNIVERSITY OF TOLEDO
History 499:10
Peace Movements in America

January 7, 1975

C.L. BeBenedetti
M-W-F 9-11 a.m.

Required readings

Brock, Peter, RADICAL PACIFISTS IN ANTEBELLUM AMERICA (Princecton paperback)

Chatfield, Charles (ed.), PEACE MOVEMENTS IN AMERICA (Shocken paperback)

Falk, Richard, et al. (eds.), CRIMES OF WAR (Vintage paperback)

Herman, Sondra, ELEVEN AGAINST WAR (Stanford paperback)

Wittner, Lawrence, REBELS AGAINST WAR (Columbia paperback)

Schedule	Readings

January

W-8   Introduction

F-10   The Anthropology of Human Aggression: Chatfield/Washburgn

M-13   Pacifism and Christianity to the 18th century.

W-15   Quakerism and the American Peace Witness, 1763-1815

F-17   The Beginnings of the Modern Peace Reform, 1815-1860: Broks, chs. 1-2,6.

M-20   Pacifism and Abolitionism: Brock, chs. 3-5, 7.

W-22   Peacekeeping and the Civil War: Brock, ch. 8 and epilogue.

F-24   The Ingathering Peace Movement, 1865-90.

M-27   The Anti-Imperialist Movement, 1898-1904: Chatfield/ Gianakos.

W-29   International Law as the International Reform, 1865-1914: Herman, chs. 1-2.

F-31   Peace as the Respectable Reform: Herman, chs. 4-6; Chatfield/Patterson.

February

M-3   The Internationalist Crisis, 1914-21: Herman, chs. 3,7, and Afterword.

W-5   World War I and American Pacifism: Chatfield/Cook

F-7   American Peaceseeking in the 1920s: Chatfield/DeBenedetti.

W-10   Mid-term examination: inclusive to Friday, Feb. 7.

W-12   Resisting the 1930s: Chatfield/Chatfield; Robinson; Wittner, ch. 1.

F-14   World War II and American Peace Action: Wittner, chs. 2-4.

M-17   Rest

W-19   World War II and the Problem of Evil

F-21   Peace Workers and the Bomb: Wittner, ch. 5

M-24   The American Peace Movement, 1945-1960: Wittner, chs. 6-10; Chatfield/Yoder, Peterson, and Wilensky.

W-26   The Ghandian Transferal

F-28   Anti-Interventionism of the 1960s

March

M-3   The Vietnamization of Amrican Life
W-5   On Crimes of War: Falk <u>et al</u>.
F-7   The Pentagon State

M-10   Some Alternative Futures: World Order Models Project and the
           Politics of Planet Earth.
W-12   The Possibilities of Nonviolent Resistance.
F-14   The American Peace Movement as Past and Future.

Fall, 1982

Michael Zuckerman

HISTORY 700
Tradition and Modernity

September 8

Introduction

Introductory Seminar
for Graduate Students in History

September 15

Ruth Benedict, "Continuities and Discontinuities in Cultural
Conditioning," Psychiatry 1 (1938), 161-7
Pierre Bourdieu, "The Attitude of the Algerian Peasant toward
Time," in J. A. Pitt-Rivers, ed., Mediterranean Countrymen,
pp. 55-72
George Foster, "Peasant Society and the Image of Limited Good,"
American Anthropologist 67 (1965), 293-315
Clifford Geertz, "Person, Time, and Conduct in Bali," in The
Interpretation of Cultures, pp. 360-411
Clifford Geertz, "Deep Play: Notes on the Balinese Cockfight,"
in The Interpretation of Cultures, pp. 412-53
A. Irving Hallowell, "Ojibwa Ontology, Behavior, and World-View,"
in Stanley Diamond, ed., Primitive Views of the World, pp.
49-82
June Nash, "The Logic of Behavior: Curing in a Maya Indian Town,"
Human Organization 26 (1967), 132-9
Robert Redfield, "The Social Organization of Tradition," in
Peasant Society and Culture, pp. 40-59
Victor Turner, "A Ndembu Doctor in Practice," in The Forest of
Symbols, pp. 359-93
Eric Wolf, "Closed Corporate Peasant Communities in MesoAmerica
and Central Java," Southwestern Journal of Anthropology 13
(1957), 1-18

September 22

Talcott Parsons, et al., eds., Theories of Society, pp. 191-201
(Tonnies), pp. 208-13 and 436-43 (Durkheim), pp. 315-8 (Cooley),
and pp. 331-47 (Schmalenbach)
Robert Merton, "Patterns of Influence: Local and Cosmopolitan
Influentials," in Social Theory and Social Structure
C. E. Black, The Dynamics of Modernization, pp. 1-34
Samuel Huntington, "The Change to Change: Modernization, Develop-
ment, and Politics," Comparative Politics 3 (1971), 283-98
W. W. Rostow, The Stages of Economic Growth, pp. 1-35

September 29

Emmanuel LeRoy Ladurie, Montaillou
Emmanuel LeRoy Ladurie, "Motionless History," Social Science
History 1 (1977), 115-36

October 6

Fernand Braudel, The Mediterranean and the Mediterranean World
in the Age of Philip II, pp. 13-102, 138-67, 231-67, 276-95,
312-461, 657-756, 892-903, 1238-44

October 13

    Max Weber, <u>The Protestant Ethic and the Spirit of Capitalism</u>
    Keith Thomas, <u>Religion and the Decline of Magic</u>, ch. 1, 21, 22

October 20

    E. P. Thompson, "Time, Work-Discipline, and Industrial Capital-
      ism," <u>Past and Present</u> 38 (1967), 56-97
    E. P. Thompson, "The Moral Economy of the English Crowd in the
      Eighteenth Century," <u>Past and Present</u> 50 (1971), 76-136
    Edmund Morgan, "The Labor Problem at Jamestown, 1607-1618,"
      <u>American Historical Review</u> 76 (1971), 596-611
    Herbert Gutman, "Work, Culture, and Society in Industrializing
      America," <u>American Historical Review</u> 78 (1973), 531-88
    Christopher Hill, <u>The World Turned Upside Down</u>, ch. 1-2, 16-18
    Marcus Rediker, "'Under the Banner of King Death': The Social
      World of Anglo-American Pirates, 1716-1726," <u>William and Mary
      Quarterly</u> 38 (1981), 203-27

October 27

    Philippe Aries, Centuries of Childhood

November 3

    David Landes, The Unbound Prometheus, pp. 1-358

November 10

    Karl Marx, "Preface" to <u>The Critique of Political Economy</u>
    Karl Marx, <u>Pre-Capitalist Economic Formations</u>
    Karl Marx, <u>Manifesto of the Communist Party</u>
    Karl Marx, <u>The Eighteenth Brumaire of Louis Bonaparte</u>
    Karl Marx, "The British Rule in India" (on reserve)
    Andre Gunder Frank, <u>Latin America: Underdevelopment or Revolu-
      tion?</u>, ch. 1

November 17

    Reinhard Bendix, "Tradition and Modernity Reconsidered," <u>Com-
      parative Studies in Society and History</u> 9 (1967), 292-346
    Daniel Calhoun, "Participation versus Coping" (on reserve)
    Raymond Grew, "Modernization and its Discontents," <u>American
      Behavioral Scientist</u> 12 (1977), 289-312
    Alan Macfarlane, <u>The Origins of English Individualism</u>
    Lloyd and Susanne Rudolph, <u>The Modernity of Tradition</u>, pp. 3-14
    Dean Tipps, "Modernization Theory and the Comparative Study of
      Societies: A Critical Perspective," <u>Comparative Studies in
      Society and History</u> 15 (1973)
    E. A. Wrigley, "The Process of Modernization and the Industrial
      Revolution in England," <u>Journal of Interdisciplinary History</u>
      3 (1972), 225-59
    Michael Zuckerman, "Dreams that Men Dare to Dream: The Role of
      Ideas in Western Modernization," <u>Social Science History</u> 2 (1978),
      332-45

December 1

David McClelland, <u>The Achieving Society</u>, ch. 1-4, 10
Alex Inkeles and David Smith, <u>Becoming Modern</u>, ch. 1-3, 6-8,
9-12, 18-21
Stanley Bailis, "Individuals Coping: Modernization and Habitual
Change," in Harold Sharlin, ed., <u>The Freedoms of Enterprise</u>
(forthcoming) (on reserve)

December 8

Frederick Jackson Turner, "The Significance of the Frontier in
American History," in <u>The Frontier in American History</u>
Louis Hartz, <u>The Founding of New Societies</u>, ch. 1
Bernard Bailyn, <u>Education in the Forming of American Society</u>,
pp. 3-49
James Henretta, <u>The Evolution of American Society, 1700-1815</u>
James Henretta, "Families and Farms: Mentalite in Pre-Industrial
America," <u>William and Mary Quarterly</u> 35 (1978), 3-32
Michael Zuckerman, "The Fabrication of Identity in Early America,"
<u>William and Mary Quarterly</u> 34 (1977), 183-214

HERBERT H. LEHMAN COLLEGE
OF THE CITY UNIVERSITY OF NEW YORK

Martin Bauml Duberman   Spring, 1982

On Being Gay: Sexual 'Deviance', Contemporary and Historical

CONTEMPORARY

I.   Definitions: What constitutes "normal" (or, oppositely, "deviant")
     sexual Behavior?

II. Gay Lifestyle(s) and Culture
     The following is a partial listing of possible topics; others may
     be added:
     a) Is there a definable gay subculture(s)? If so, what are its
         distinctive features? Which are of special significance,
         uniqueness? (Some possibilities to explore: attitudes towards
         traditional sex roles, friendship, mating, lust; forms of
         expression -- language, art, music, theater; gay organizations
         and institutions -- the gay press, gay churches, gay male bars
         and baths, businesses, social and political groupings, the
         "ghetto".)

     b) The relationship between lesbian women and gay men. How much
         do they really share in common -- beyond same gender sexual/
         affectional orientation? Is it more accurate to speak of two
         gay lifestyles (one lesbian, one gay male), given their many
         differences in perspective?
           Discussion will focus on the following crucial issues about
         which lesbian women and gay men often (not always) disagree:
         1.   "boy-love" (cross-generational sex)
         2.   pornography
         3.   sado-masochism (S/M), plus other "kinky", "far-out"
              sexual practices (eg. "fisting")
         4.   "public" sex (the gay male penchant for "anonymous,"
              "promiscuous" sex in such places as parks, piers, subway
              johns, baths, porno theaters, back-room bars)
         5.   hustling (prostitution)
         6.   transvestism
         7.   trans-sexualism
         8.   bisexuality
         9.   lesbian separatism/gay male sexism and anti-feminism
         10. disagreement over the meaning and acceptability of such
              styles as machismo/androgyny or "butch"/"femme"

III. "Gay Power": The Political Movement
     The following is a partial list of possible topics:
     a. Is "Gay Power" a reality -- or a media invention?
     b. To the extent "Gay Power" is a reality, what forms has it
         taken? How has it expressed itself? What modes of political
         organization and strategies have been used -- and to gain what
         ends?
     c. Which gay political organizations are currently dominant?
     d. Do they differ in strategies and goals? Do they cooperate or
         compete with one another?

147

e. Are they different -- in tactics, goals and constituencies -- from the political groupings (eg: Gay Liberation Front; The Furies) that dominated the movement at its inception (1970)?

f. Currently (1982) the National Gay Task Force is probably the best known political organization and The Advocate, the publication with the largest gay (male) circulation. Who do they claim to represent? Who do they actually represent? Is it true, for example (as is often charged), that currently the "gay movement" is dominated by white, young, middle-class men? And that only a small percentage of even that group is politically active?

g. If so -- why?
Are the "established" gay political organizations exclusionary - consciously or unconsciously racist, classist, ageist and sexist?
Are Third World gays politically involved? Working-class gays? Rural gays?
Do lesbian women have their own organizations? Do they ever work together politically with gay men -- and if so, within what groups and around what particular issues?
If (as seems the case) most gay people are politically uninvolved, is the reason fear (still closeted; afraid for their jobs; isolated in small towns) or hedonism (absorbed in discos, drugs and sex)?

h. The Gay Left: "Civil Rights" Are Not Enough
The key question here is evaluating the gay left's charge that a movement radical at its inception (in its challenge to traditional sex role stereotyping and sexual behavior) has been taken over by mainstream middle-class whites whose orientation is"reformist": winning acceptance from mainstream American by proving they're "'jes folks'", dominated by the values of capitalist consumerism and concerned solely with civil rights legislation (not substantive social change). Even if the indictment gay radicals have made of the "official" Gay Movement is accurate, what conclusions follow therefrom? For example, is the gay left (socialist and anarchist) deluded in thinking anything more than "reformism" is possible in this country?

i. The reaction of the traditional liberal/radical ("straight") Left to the gay rights movement. Why have so few offered support -- in contrast to the large numbers who rallied behind the Black civil rights movement and the anti-Vietnam war movement?

IV. The Gay Backlash
a. The nature of "homophobia". Who are those most hostile to gay people -- and why? Do they share a particular set of values and/or fit a particular personality profile?

Among the topics to be discussed in trying to answer the above question is:
1) the role of organized religion
2) the Anita Bryant and Jerry Falwell anti-gay crusades
3) the gay "threat" (real or imagined) to the nuclear family, to monogamous lifetime pair-bonding and to sharply differentiated male and female "roles"

4) the emotional/psychological components of homophobia, often tangled/unacknowledged/contradictory. For example, the mix of envy, fear and disgust in a traditionally sex-negative country to the variety of gay sexual "practices" and partners, the "instability" of gay relationships and the "irresponsibility" of not rearing children

5) the particular issues most often stressed by the anti-gay backlash: whether admitted homosexuals should be allowed to teach, serve in the armed forces, become citizens, be given custody of their own children -- or be allowed to adopt.

POSTSCRIPT:

Given the limited time available to us in a single term, we'll be lucky if we manage to discuss with sufficient depth and detail the bewildering variety of questions and issues outined in PARTS I-IV. To expect more would be unrealistic.

But I do want you to be aware that the subjects described in PARTS I-IV hardly exhaust the range of possibilities. The topic of "sexual 'deviance'" has vast ramifications, and can be illuminated by insights derived from the study of an equally vast range of disciplines -- from poetry to medicine to law. And above all (I'm probably prejudiced here) from a study of history.

If time permits (which seems unlikely) we will move on from contemporary issues to theoretical and historical ones. It's inevitable in any case that we will discuss some theory and history this term. It would be impossible, for example, when discussing the phenomenon of bisexuality today to avoid its historical manifestations -- in ancient Greece, say -- or fail to evaluate the many theories (derived from disciplines as varied as psychology, sociology and anthropology) for "explaining" it.

Next term (Fall '84), I hope to shift the course's focus. Since this semester our attention will be almost entirely on "being gay" in its contemporary setting, next time around I'll concentrate on historical and theoretical perspectives.

To give you some awareness of the data and insights that can be derived from the social and behavioral sciences:

1. from psychology: the theoretical perspectives of (among others) Ulrichs, Krafft-Ebing, Freud, Havelock Ellis, Kinsey, Masters and Johnson.

2. from anthropology: patterns and "norms" of sexual behavior in "primitive" cultures so markedly different from ours as to force a re-examination of the presumed "universality" of our own mores.

3. from sociology: the nature of "role-playing"; the formation and functions of "subcultures"; the effect of group norms on individual needs.

4. from political theory: the role of the State in defining and controlling "acceptable" sexual behavior; the significance of "community".

5. from biology (and sociobiology): the genetic and hormonal substrata that may play a role in determining sexual and affectional preferences.

6. from animal (and especially primate) studies: "dominance" theory; the importance of "instincts" (if any); the link (if any) between "innate" aggression and patterns of sexual behavior.

And so on .....

I think I've made my point: we're embarking on a study of certain long-ignored yet crucially important aspects of human experience. The field is new; the amount of information all at once fragmentary, vast and contradictory; "answers" hard to come by. Strap on your hiking boots -- it's difficult terrain. and challenging.

****

READINGS

No satisfactory "text" exists. I will hand out materials xeroxed from a variety of sources (scholarly journals, the gay press, chapters from books, etc.) to cover the topics we discuss.

For those seeking additional information, I have drawn up the following bibliography as a guide. It lists many of the "best" titles currently available-- but keep in mind that the choice is subjective (mine) and that even the "best," in an infant discipline, is far from being comprehensive.

A. <u>Books</u>:

Dennis Altman, THE HOMOSEXUALIZATION OF AMERICA (St. Martin's: 1982)
John Boswell, CHRISTIANITY, SOCIAL TOLERANCE AND HOMOSEXUALITY (Chi.: '82)
Margaret Cruikshank, LESBIAN STUDIES (Feminist Press: '82)
K.J. Dover, GREEK HOMOSEXUALITY (Harvard: '78)
Lillian Faderman, SURPASSING THE LOVE OF MEN (Morrow: '81)
Jeanette Foster, SEX VARIANT WOMEN IN LITERATURE (the classic bibliographic work,
     reprinted by Diana Press in '75)
Jonathan Katz, GAY AMERICAN HISTORY (Crowell: '76)
Sydney Abbott and Barbara Love, SAPPHO WAS A RIGHT-ON WOMAN
Cheri Moraga, ed., THIS BRIDGE CALLED OUR BACKS (third world women)
Jan Morris, CONUNDRUM (trans-sexualism; firsthand acct.)
Masters and Johnson, HOMOSEXUALITY IN PERSPECTIVE (Little, Brown: '79)
Gay Left Collective, HOMOSEXUAL POWER AND POLITICS (Allison & Busby: '80)
C. Tripp, THE HOMOSEXUAL MATRIX (McGraw-Hill: '75)
Judith Schwarz, THE RADICAL FEMINISTS OF HETERODOXY (New Victoria Press: '82)
SEXUALITY IN HISTORY (special issue of THE RADICAL HISTORY REVIEW: '79)
HISTORICAL PERSPECTIVES ON HOMOSEXUALITY (special issue of THE JOURNAL OF
     HOMOSEXUALITY: '80-'81)
Judith Schwarz, ed., special issue of FRONTIERS (Fall, '79) on Lesbian History
J.H. Roberts, BLACK LESBIANS: AN ANNOTATED BIBLIOGRAPHY (Naiad: '81)
Daniel Tasng, ed., THE AGE TABOO (Allyson: '81); on "boy love" (excellent
     bibliography)
Janice Raymond, THE TRANSEXUAL EMPIRE (excellent bibliography)
Jeffrey Weeks, COMING OUT: HOMOSEXUAL POLITICS IN BRITAIN IN THE 19TH CENTURY
     TO THE PRESENT (Quartet: '77)
Winston Leyland, ed., THE 'GAY SUNSHINE' INTERVIEWS, 2 vols, '78-'82; The Gay
     Sunshine Press
Ed White, STATES OF DESIRE (essays on contemporary gay life across the U.S.)
Deborah Wolf, THE LESBIAN COMMUNITY (University of California)
**(The fullest bibliography on all subjects -- plus fiction, which is not
included in this list -- is THE WHOLE GAY CATALOGUE, Lambda Rising: '82)

B. Articles:

Pat Califia, "Lesbian S/M," THE ADVOCATE, Dec. 27, 1979 (see, too, her COMING
    TO POWER: Samois Press)
Larry Busch, "The NewSeparatism," CHRISTOPHER STREET, Aug. '81
Martin Bauml Duberman, "Bisexuality," NEW TIMES, June 28, '74
_____ _____, THE NEW YORK NATIVE, '81-'83, column on gay and lesbian
    history entitled "About Time"
Robert Oaks, "Things Fearful to Name," JOURNAL OF SOCIAL HISTORY (17th Century
    New England)
Nancy Sahli, "Smashing: Women's Relationships Before the Fall," CHRYSALLIS,
    8:17-27
R. Trumback, "London's Sodomites," JOURNAL OF SOCIAL HISTORY, Fall '77 (contains
    excellent bibliography)
Kenneth Sherrill, "Homophobia: Illness or Disease," '74 (excellent bibliography)
Ellen Willis, article on pornography, THE VILLAGE VOICE, Oct. 15, '79
"Lesbian Culture," WIN (entire issue), June 26, '75
Joan Nestle, "Butch-Fem in the '50s," HERESIES (periodical put out by The
    Heresies Collective), SEX ISSUE (the whole of this issue worth reading)
Vern Bullough, "Transsexualism In History," ARCH. S.B. '75
_____, "Transvestites in the Middle Ages," AJS
Peter Fontaine, "Gay Life in Africa," NEW GAY LIFE, May '78
Adrienne Rich, "Compulsive Heterosexuality and Lesbian Existence," SIGNS, v. 5, '80

To sample anti-gay views: Norman Podhoretz, "The Cult of Appeasement," HARPER'S,
                        Oct. '77
                        Midge Decter, "The Boys...Beach", COMMENTARY, S. '80
                        E. Sagarin, lengthy review of varied books,
                        CONTEMPORARY SOCIOLOGY, Jan. '73

C. Periodicals:

Among the leading gay male and lesbian female magazines, newspapers and journals:

THE BODY POLITIC (Toronto; radical/socialist); THE ADVOCATE (largest circulation;
"centrist" views); CHRISTOPHER STREED (literary); THE NEW YORK NATIVE; GAY NEWS
(Phil.); BLADE (D.C.); JOURNAL OF HOMOSEXUALITY (scholarly); FAG RAG (Boston;
radical/anarchist); LESBIAN TIDE; CONDITIONS (journal); OFF OUR BACKS (national);
CHRYSALLIS (scholarly); WOMEN'S NEWS

For periodicals no longer in print, see Jonathan Katz, ed., LESBIAN AND GAY MEN
IN HISTORY AND LITERATURE, Arno Press: '75, 54 vols. (For example, the series
contains reprints of the full run of two historic publications: (a) THE LADDER
(lesbian; 1956-'72); (b) MATTACHINE (1955-'66)

Seminar   Dr. Walter Williams
October 9 - November 13, 1980   Associate Professor of History
Thursday 7:30 - 9:30 p.m.   University of Cincinnati
$30.00 Registration   475-4538 or 221-8092

SEXUAL VARIANCE IN HISTORY

This class will focus on the various attitudes toward and manifestations of homosexuality in world cultures, from ancient times to the present. It is designed for lesbians and gay men who are concerned about their own group's place in history, as well as non-gays who may wish to learn about this ignored aspect of the human story. Class discussion will be encouraged and each member of the class will be strongly encouraged (but not required) to lead a part of a class discussion on one topic from the readings.

GENERAL

Text: Vern Bullough, Sexual Variance in Society and History
      Jeanette Foster, Sex Variant Women in Literature
      Jane Rule, Lesbian Images: Biographies
      Special Lesbian History Issue, Frontiers: A Journal of Women's
        Studies (Fall 1979)
      Byrne R.S. Fone, ed., Hidden Heritage: History and the Gay Imagination
        (Men)
      Delores Klaitch, Woman Plus Woman: Attitudes Toward Lesbianism
      Special History Issue, Journal of Homosexuality (Fall 1980)
      Vern Bullough, et.al., An Annotated Bibliography of Homosexuality
      Barbara Gittings, A Gay Bibliography: American Library Association

TRADITIONAL NON-WESTERN CULTURES

Topics: Evolutionary Background, American Indians, Asia, Oceania, Africa,
        Middle East.

      Jonathan Katz, Gay American History (Section on North American Indians)
      Donald Webster Cory, ed., Homosexuality: A Cross Cultural Approach
      Wainwright Churchill, Homosexual Behavior Among Males: A Cross Cultural
        and Cross Species Investigation
      Saikaker Ihara, Comrade Loves of the Samurai (trans. from Japanese by
        E.P. Mathers)
      C.S. Ford ane F.A. Beach, Patterns of Sexual Behavior (chapter on
        homosexuality)
      Vern Bullough, Sexual Variance in Society and History (Middle East, India
        and China chapters)
      Human Relations Area Files "Category, 838: Homosexuality"
      Maggie Childs, "Japan's Homosexual Heritage," Gai Saber I (Spring 1977):
        41-45.

ANCIENT MEDITERRANEAN

Topics: Greece and Rome, Hebrews, Christian Rome and Medieval

      Tom Horner, Jonathan Lloyd David: Homosexuality in Biblical Times

Derrick Sherwin Bailey, Homosexuality and the Western Christian
    Tradition (Hebrews, Cristian Rome and Medieval)
Thomas Szasz, The Manufacture of Madness: A Comparative Study of the
    Inquisition and the Mental Health Movement
G. Legman, The Guilt of the Templars (for Medieval Specialists)
K.J. Dover, Greek Homosexuality
J. Ungaretti, "Pederast, Heroism, and the Family in Classical Greece,"
    Journal of Homosexuality 3 (1978): 291-300
Sarah Pomeroy, Goddesses, Whores, Wives, and Slaves: Women in Classical
    Antiquity (1975)
Douglas Roby, "Early Medieval Attitudes Toward Nomosexuality," Gai Saber I
    (Spring 1977): 67-71
Michael Goodich, The Unmentionable Vice: Homosexuality in the Late
    Medieval Period
John Boswell, Christianity and the Toleration of Homosexuality

EUROPE 1000-1940

Topics: Late Middle Ages and Renaissance (rise of urban subculture, artists,
       court subcultures in Italy and France): Reformation and early Modern
       Europe (court subcultures: William II of England, Richard II of England,
       Henri III of France, James I of England, Christine of Sweden, Louis XIV
       of France, Frederick the Great of Prussia; French revolution and
       Napoleonic Code); English gay subculture 1700-1940; German gay movement
       1860-1940; Russia 1900-1940; Literary Lesbians in Paris, 1900-1940.

Georgina Masson, Queen Christina (1968)
Susan Henderson "Frederick the Great of Prussia," Gai Saber I (Spring 1977):
    46-54
Louie Crew, ed., The Gay Academic (chapter on Europena history)
Randolph Trumback "London's Sodomites: 18th Century," Journal of
    Social History (Fall 1977): 1-33
H. Montgomery Hyde, The Love that Dared Not Speak its Name (England)
H. Montgomery Hyde, The Trials of Oscar Wilde
H. Montgomery Hyde, The Cleveland Street Scandal (England)
Jeffrey Weeks, Coming Out: Homosexual Politics in Britain from the 19th
    Century to the Present
A.L. Rowse, Homosexuals in History (gossipy and outdated)
Brian Reade, ed., Sexual Heretics: Male Homosexuality in English
    Literature 1850-1900
James Steakley, The Homosexual Emancipation Movement in Germany
John Lauritsen and David Thorstad, The Early Homosexual Rights Movement
    1864-1900
John Stewart Collis, Havelock Ellis (1959)
Christopher Isherwood, Christopher and His Kind, 1929-1939 (Germany)
Rupert Croft-Cooke, The Unrecorded Life of Oscar Wilde (1972) (England)
Phyllis Grosskurth, The Woeful Victorian: A Biography of John Addington
    Symonds (England)
Alan Bray, Homosexuality in Renaissance England, Gay Men's Press,
    P.O. Box 247, London N 15, 6RW 7.95

Quentin Bell, <u>Virginia Woolf</u>, (1974)
Mary Louisa Gordon, <u>The Chase of the Wild Goose</u> (1936) (Biography on the
   English "Ladies of Llangollen")
Radclyffe Hall, <u>The Well of Lonliness</u> (1929) (English lesbian fictional
   autobirgraphy)
Elizabeth Manor, <u>The Ladies of Llangollen: A Study in Romantic Friendship</u>
   (1971) (biography of 18th Century English female coupel, bu no overt
   lesbian theme)
Nigel Nicolson, <u>Portrait of a Marriage</u> (1973) (biography of English
   bisexual writers, Vita Sackville-West and her husband, Harold Nicolson)
Mary Sturgeon, <u>Michael Field</u> (1921) (biography of late 1800 lesbian
   poets who used a male pseudonym)

THE PARIS SCENE

George Wickes, <u>The Amazon of Letters: The Life and Loves of Natalie Barney</u>
   (A Cincinnati expatriate Lesbian in Paris)
Jean Chalon, <u>Portrait of a Seductress: The World of Natalie Barney</u>
Margaret Anderson, <u>My Thirty Years War</u> (1930); <u>Fiery Foundations</u> (1951);
   and <u>Strange Necessity</u> (1970) (autobiography of expatriate publisher, and
   her relationships in Paris with Jane Heap, Georgette Leblanc and
   Dorothy Caruso)
Sylvia Beach, <u>Shakespeare and Company</u> (1956) (autobiography of a Paris
   lesbian who ran a bookshop for U.S. expatriates)
Kay Boyle and Robert McAlmon, <u>Being Geniuses Together</u>, 1920-1930 (1968)
   (Gay Paris expatriates)
Richard Bridgeman, <u>Gertrude Stein in Pieces</u> (1970)
Sidonie Colette, <u>Earthly Paradise</u> (1966) (autobiography of her relationships
   with Renee Vivien and LaChevaliere in Paris)
Sidonie Colette, <u>The Pure and the Impure</u> (1933) (Essay on homosexual love,
   on Renee Vivien and the English "Ladies of Llangollen")
Samuel Edwards, <u>George Sand</u> (1972) (bisexual French woman writer)
Janet Flanner, <u>Paris was Yesterday, 1925-1954</u> (1963)
Comptom MacKenzie, <u>Extraordinary Women: Theme and Variations</u> (1928)
   (gay life on island of Capri in 1920's)
Andre Maurois, <u>Lelia: The Life of George Sand</u> (1954)
Robert Phelps, <u>Sidonie Gabriella Colette, 1873-1954</u> (1963)
Alice B. Toklas, <u>Staying on Alone</u> (1973) (her Paris relationship with
   Gertrude Stein)
Alice B. Tolkas, <u>What is Remembered</u> (1963) (ditto)
Alice B. Toklas, <u>Autobiography of Alice B. Toklas</u>
Irving Drutman, ed., <u>Janet Flanner's World</u>

UNITED STATES TO 1940

Topics: 18th Century laws, men on the frontier, women before 1940, medical
         attitudes, literary aspects, rise of an urban gay subculture.

Jonathan Katz, ed., <u>Gay American History</u>
Robert K. Martin, <u>The Homosexual Tradition in American Poetry</u>

Roger Austen, Playing the Game: The Homosexual Novel in America
Esther Newton, Mother Camp: Female Impersonators in America
Paula Bennett, "The Language of Love: Emily Dickenson's Homoerotic
    Poetry," Gai Saber I (Spring 1977): 13-17
Isabel Miller, Patience and Sarah (1972) (fictionalized biography of
    1820's U.S. painters, Mary Ann Willson and Sarah Brundidge
Rebecca Patterson, The Riddle of Emily Dickinson (1951)
John Cody, After Great Pain: Emily Dickinson (1971) (Chapter 3)

GAY AND LESBIAN RIGHTS MOVEMENT SINCE 1940

Topics: (1950-1969) Homophibe movement, Lesbian Organizations; (1969-present)
    Gay Liberations, Lesbian Feminism; effects of the movement on medical,
    religious, and legal institutions.

Vitto Russo, The Celluloid Closet (homophobic movies)
John Gerassi, The Boys of Boise (homophobia 1950's)
Arthur Bell, Dancing the Gay Lib Blues (New York early 1970s)
Howard Brown, Familiar Faces, Hidden Lives: Homosexual Men in America Today
Ruth Simpson, From the Closet to the Courts: The Lesbian Transition
Sidney Abbott and Barbara Love, Sappho Was a Right-On Woman
Laud Humphreys, Out of the Closets
Don Teal, The Gay Militants (1969-1970)
Troy Perry, The Lord is my Shepherd and He Knows I'm Gay
Deborah Goleman Wolf, The Lesbian Community
N. Myron and C. Bunch, eds., Lesbianism and the Women's Movement
Karla Jay and Allen Young, eds., Out of the Closets
Karla Jay and Allen Young, eds., After You're Out
Karla Jay and Allen Young, eds., Lavender Culture
Wardell Pomeroy, Dr. Kinsey and the Institute for Sex Research
Del Martin and Phyllis Lyon, Lesbian/Women
Sasha G. Lewis, Sunday's Women: Lesbian Life Today

155

MOUNT HOLYOKE COLLEGE
Department of History

History 381 American Media in the Twentieth Century   Daniel J. Czitrom
Fall, 1983   641 Library
Tel: 538-2446(o)
536-5277(h)

This is a research seminar in the history of the media in recent America.
It is both necessary and desirable for us to dip into criticism, sociology,
psychology, philosophy, and communications theory along the way. But while
these are all grist for our mill I want to emphasize that this will be a
history course. The evolution of communication forms and content <u>over time</u>
seems to me the center of our inquiry. Two important parallel themes: how
have our efforts to comprehend media developed, and how have new media themselves changed the way we think and feel.

> "The service rendered by intoxicating media in the struggle for
> happiness and in keeping misery at a distance is so highly prized
> as a benefit that individuals and peoples alike have given them an
> established place in the economics of their libido. We owe to such
> media not merely the immediate yield of pleasure, but also a
> greatly desired degree of independence from the external world."
>
> -- S. Freud, CIVILIZATION AND ITS DISCONTENTS

BOOKS TO PURCHASE: (Odyssey Bookstore)

Michael Schudson, DISCOVERING THE NEWS
Daniel J. Czitrom, MEDIA AND THE AMERICAN MIND
Robert Sklar, MOVIE MADE AMERICA
Erik Barnouw, THE SPONSOR
Todd Gitlin, THE WHOLE WORLD IS WATCHING
Seminar Packet

COURSE REQUIREMENTS:

1) Research Project-- Each student will be expected to write a carefully
conceived analytical research paper exploring some aspect of media history.
You will be expected to take full advantage of the primary and secondary
sources available in the Five College collections. Paper outlines and
preliminary bibliographies will be due November 8. I have reserved the last
two weeks of class time for group discussion of the projects. Completed
projects due the last day of classes.

2) Journals-- We will all keep a reflective Journal during the semester to
record our thoughts, insights, questions, rage, delight, etc. <u>viz.</u> the
media today. I am purposely leaving the subject wide open. You may choose
to comment on any single facet of current media fare; you may want to focus
on one medium, or you may be comparative; you might tie some of the readings to
what you see and hear. The Journal has a double purpose: to get you thinking
about potential research topics and to get you to connect the media environment of today with what we learn about its past. From time to time
I may call on you to read aloud in class from your Journal; I will collect
the Journals at some point, too, commenting on, but not grading, them.

3) Review Essay-- Each of you will choose one book from the supplementary
reading list and write a 3-5 page critique of the work.

WEEK

1   Course Introduction
Discussion Starters
Req: Daniel Boorstin, "Communication Technology For Better or Worse" Packet

2   Communication as ritual and transmission
Telegraph: Annihilation of space and time
Birth of the "penny press"
Req: James W. Carey, "A Cultural Approach to Communication" Packet
     Czitrom, Ch. 1
     Schudson, Ch. 1-2

3   News as a form of knowledge
New journalism of the 1890's
Muckraking
Req: Schudson, Ch. 3-4
     James W. Carey, "The Problem of Journalism History" Packet

4   Urban amusements and early film audiences
Motion pictures and the new popular culture
Req: Czitrom, Ch. 2
     Sklar, Part 1-2
     In class screening: D.W. Griffith, "Musketeers of Pig Alley"; Mack Sennett,
                  "Coney Island"

5   Hollywood: The religion of the movies
Film as historical evidence
Req: Sklar, Part 3-4
     Screening, 10/10, 7pm: Billy Wilder, "Double Indemnity"; "March of Time"
                        newsreel

6   Radio, the ethereal hearth
Broadcasting and advertising
Origins of the recording industry
Req: Czitrom, Ch. 3
     Barnouw, Part 1
     Stuart Ewen, "Advertising as Social Production" Packet
     Slide and tape presentation: "American Popular Music, 1920-1960", Details TBA

7   Television: Continuities and changes in broadcasting
Television and politics I: the '50's
Req: Barnouw, Part 2-3
     Raymond Williams, "The Technology and the Society" Packet
     Gitlin, Skim Part 1
     Screening, 10/31, 7pm: Emile D'Antonio, "Point of Order"

8   Television and politics II: the '60's
Req: Gitlin, Part 2
     Screening, 11/7, 7pm: Ely Landau, "King: From Montgomery to Memphis"

9   Women and minorities in the media
Cultural stereotyping
Req: Gaye Tuchman, "Women's Depiction by the Mass Media" Packet
     In class screening: John Berger, "Ways of Seeing"

10   Media and popular culture--aesthetics and history
      Req: John Cawelti, "Notes Toward An Aesthetics of Popular Culture" Packet
          David Marc, DEMOGRAPHIC VISTAS: TELEVISION AND AMERICAN CULTURE,
                Ch. 1,5 Reserve

11   Toward media theory
      Future shock: cable, satellite, videodisc, and beyond
      Req: Czitrom, Ch. 4-6, Epilogue
          Hans Magnus Enzensberger, "Constituents of A Theory of the Media" Reserve

12-13   Individual Projects

SUPPLEMENTARY READING LIST

WEEK

2: Dan Schiller, OBJECTIVITY AND THE NEWS (R)
   Edwin and Michael Emery, THE PRESS AND AMERICA (R)
   Isaac Pray, MEMOIRS OF JAMES G. BENNETT
   Victor Rosewater, HISTORY OF COOPERATIVE NEWSGATHERING IN THE US
   Gaye Tuchman, MAKING NEWS: A STUDY IN THE CONSTRUCTION OF REALITY

3: Ronald Weber, THE LITERATURE OF FACT (R)
   Tom Wolfe, ed., THE NEW JOURNALISM (R)
   Theodore Green, AMERICA'S HEROES
   Harold S. Wilson, MCCLURE'S MAGAZINE AND THE MUCKRAKERS
   Theodore Petersen, MAGAZINES IN THE TWENTIETH CENTURY
   George Juergens, JOSEPH PULITZER
   W.A. Swanberg, CITIZEN HEARST
   Lincoln Steffens, AUTOBIOGRAPHY

4: Lary May, SCREENING OUT THE PAST: THE BIRTH OF MASS CULTURE AND THE MOTION
            PICTURE INDUSTRY (R)
   Benjamin Hampton, HISTORY OF THE AMERICAN FILM INDUSTRY
   Alexander Walker, STARDOM: THE HOLLYWOOD PHENOMENON
   Hortense Powdermaker, HOLLYWOOD: THE DREAM FACTORY
   Robert Henderson, D.W. GRIFFITH

5: John O'Connor and Martin Jackson, AMERICAN HISTORY/AMERICAN FILM (R)
   Larry Ceplair and Steven Englund, THE INQUISITION IN HOLLYWOOD (R)
   Raymond Fielding, THE MARCH OF TIME
   Marjorie Rosen, POPCORN VENUS: WOMEN, MOVIES, AND THE AMERICAN DREAM

6: Erik Barnouw, A HISTORY OF BROADCASTING IN THE US, 3 VOLS. (R)
   J. Fred MacDonald, DON'T TOUCH THAT DIAL! RADIO PROGRAMMING IN AMERICAN
                    LIFE, 1920-1960

7: Horace Newcomb, ed., TELEVISION: THE CRITICAL VIEW
   Les Brown, TELEVISION: THE BUSINESS BEHIND THE BOX
   Robert Sklar, PRIME TIME AMERICA
   RED CHANNELS: THE REPORT OF COMMUNIST INFLUENCE IN RADIO AND TELEVISION

8: Marshall McLuhan, UNDERSTANDING MEDIA (R)
   Joe McGinnis, THE SELLING OF THE PRESIDENT
   Fred Friendly, DUE TO CIRCUMSTANCES BEYOND OUR CONTROL
   Herbert Gans, DECIDING WHAT'S NEWS
   Frank Mankiewicz and Joel Swerdlow, REMOTE CONTROL
   George Comstock, et. al., TELEVISION AND HUMAN BEHAVIOR

9: Gaye Tuchman, et. al., eds., HEARTH AND HOME: IMAGES OF WOMEN IN THE MASS MEDIA
   Elizabeth and Stuart Ewen, CHANNEL OF DESIRE
   George Gerbner and Nancy Signorielli, "Women and Minorities in Television Drama:
                    A Research Report" (R)

10: Marshall McLuhan, THE MECHANICAL BRIDE (R)
    Horace Newcomb, TELEVISION: THE MOST POPULAR ART
    John Cawelti, ADVENTURE, MYSTERY, ROMANCE: FORMULA STORIES AS ART AND POPULAR CULTURE
    Greil Marcus, MYSTERY TRAIN: IMAGES OF AMERICA IN ROCK'N'ROLL
    Roland Barthes, MYTHOLOGIES
    J. Hoberman and Jonathan Rosenbaum, MIDNIGHT MOVIES

SUPPLEMENTARY READING LIST

11: **Herbert Schiller,** COMMUNICATIONS AND CULTURAL DOMINANCE
        _____, MASS COMMUNICATIONS AND AMERICAN EMPIRE
   Anthony Smith, THE GEOPOLITICS OF INFORMATION
   Brenda Maddox, BEYOND BABEL

Mount Holyoke College
Department of History
Spring 1983

History 381:   REEL AMERICA: HISTORY AND FILM
Daniel Czitrom and Katherine St. Clair

"It is like writing history with lightning."
          --Woodrow Wilson after viewing "Birth of a Nation"

"Being a vast attempt to industrialize an artistic medium, Hollywood must
feed upon all sorts of digestive devices and an agglomeration of raw
materials to satisfy its mere size. It is mammoth, mammal, mammon.
Theoretically, there is nothing which the camera cannot conceive and
project on a conveniently empty screen; nothing from journalism to
Shakespeare; and there is nothing, practically, which it leaves untouched.
Hollywood cannot be choosy."
          --Parker Tyler, The Hollywood Hallucination

"I had a monumental idea this morning, but I didn't like it."
          --Samuel Goldwyn

     This seminar is an inquiry into the relationship between film and
history. We will be looking not only at the history of the movie industry
in America, but also at how movies themselves have shaped our sense of the
past. We will be paying special attention to the issue of film as
historical evidence, and the ways in which political and social conflicts
have been presented (or ignored) in Hollywood films.

     The list of movies to be studied was made within certain constraints
of budget, availability, and timing. There may be late changes from
time-to-time. All films will be screened on Tuesday nights, 7:30pm, in
either Hooker (H), Andreola Room (A), or Wiese-Meriwether Room (W-M).

COURSE REQUIREMENTS:

1)Film Journal-- Each student will be expected to keep a journal of all the
films she has seen during the semester, both in and out of class. Journal
entries ought to be in the form of thoughtful (and informal) reflections on
films and/or relevant readings. The journals should also be the place
where students work toward developing their final paper topic.
Occasionally, students will be asked to read from their journals in class.
The journals will be collected twice during the semester.

2)Discussion Starter-- Each student will be responsible for leading the
discussion for two films during the course. Discussion starters will be
expected to do a bit of supplementary reading and research to shed further
light on the film being considered that week.

3)Final Paper-- An in-depth research project on some aspect of film and
history, utilizing both primary and secondary sources. You may decide to
write on one (or several) individual films, on some episode in film history
(e.g. business, regulation, censorship), on the work of an auteur, on a
recurring social or political issue, on the treatment of a specific
historical theme-- these are merely a few of the possibilities. Papers
will be due May 6; a rough draft will be expected some time before that.

REQUIRED TEXTS: (Odyssey Bookstore)
Robert Sklar, Movie- Made America
Molly Haskell, From Reverence to Rape
Dashiell Hammett, The Maltese Falcon
James M. Cain, Mildred Pierce
Seminar Packet (History Office, 205 Library)

ON RESERVE:
Film & History
Mary Beth Norton, et al., A People and a Nation, Vol. II

SCHEDULE

Week	Films	Reading
2/1	In class: Lumiere compilation; Melies compilation; E. Porter, "The Great Train Robbery" (1903)	
2/8	D.W. Griffith, "A Corner in Wheat" (1909) and "Musketeers of Pig Alley" (1912); M. Sennett, "Tillie's Punctured Romance" (1914), "Cast Adrift" (1917), "Coney Island" (1917) (A)	Sklar, Ch.1-4 J. Agee, "Comedy's Greatest Era" J. O'Connor and M. Jackson, "Introduction" to American History /American Film Moving Picture World, 1907-1915 (microfilm)
2/15	D.W. Griffith, "Birth of a Nation" (1915) (H)	Sklar, Ch.5-9 NAACP,"Fighting a Vicious Film" D.W. Griffith,"The Rise and Fall of Free Speech in America"
2/22	W. Wellman, "Public Enemy" (1931) (A)	Sklar, Ch.10-11 G. Jowett, "Public Enemy" R. Warshow, "The Gangster as Tragic Hero"
3/1	M. LeRoy,"I am A Fugitive from A Chain Gang" (1932) (A)	Sklar, Ch.12-14 A. Bergman, "Warner Bros. Presents Social Consciousness" R. Moley, "Birth of MPPA Code" and MPPA Code
3/8	B. Berkeley, "Goldiggers of 1933" (1933); Workers Film and Photo League Compilation (1930-1935) (A)	Haskell, pp.1-41; 90-152 W. Stott, Documentary Expression and Thirties America, Ch.1-3
3/15	M. Curtiz, "Mildred Pierce" (1942) (A)	Haskell, pp.153-230 Cain, Mildred Pierce
3/29	O. Welles, "Citizen Kane" (1941); March of Time Newsreel (W-M)	P. Wollen, "The Auteur Theory" D Bordwell,"Citizen Kane"

4/5	J. Huston, "The Maltese Falcon" (1941) (H)	D. Hammett, <u>The Maltese Falcon</u> P. Shrader, "Notes on Film Noir"
4/10	Special Screening: "Hollywood on Trial" (1975) (H)	
4/12	A. Polonsky, "Force of Evil" (1946) (A)	V. Navasky, <u>Naming Names,</u> Ch. 4-6 A. Polonsky interview Sklar, Ch. 15-16
4/19	R. Brooks, "Blackboard Jungle" (1955) (H)	Sklar, Ch. 17-18 R. Staehling, "The Truth About Teen Movies"
4/26	J. Ford, "The Searchers" (1956)	Dossier on John Ford R. Warshow, "The Westerner"
5/3	K. Anger, "Scorpio Rising" (1964) (A)	

REEL AMERICA: (A VERY) SELECTED BIBLIOGRAPHY

GENERAL HISTORIES
Kenneth Anger, Hollywood Bablyon
Benjamin Hampton, History of the American Film Industry
Lewis Jacobs, The Rise of American Film
Garth Jowett, Film: The Democratic Art
Gerald Mast, ed., The Movies in Our Midst
John O'Connor and Martin Jackson, eds., American History/American
    Film: Interpreting the Hollywood Image
Paul Smith, ed., THE HISTORIAN AND FILM

GENERAL CRITICISM
Dudley Andrew, Major Film Theories
Richard Corliss, Talking Pictures: Screenwriters in the American
    Cinema
David Denby, ed., Awake in the Dark
Charles Flynn and Todd McCarthy, eds., Kings of the B's: Working
    Within the Hollywood System
J.Hoberman and Jonathan Rosenbaum, Midnight Movies
Bill Nichols, ed., Movies and Methods
Andrew Sarris, American Cinema
Parker Tyler, The Hollywood Hallucination

EARLY FILM
Kevin Brownlow, The Parade's Gone By
_____, Hollywood: The First Twenty Years
C.W. Ceram, The Archaeology of the Cinema
William K. Everson, American Silent Film
John Fell, Film and the Narrative Tradition
Harry Geduld, ed., Focus on D.W. Griffith
Robert Henderson, D.W. Griffith: His Life and Work
Donald McCaffrey, ed., Focus on Chaplin
Kenneth MacGowan, Behind the Screen
Gerald Mast, The Comic Mind
Lary May, Screening Out the Past: The Birth of Mass Culture and
    the Motion Picture Industry
Kemp Niver, The First Twenty Years
Anthony Slide, Early American Cinema
Edward Wagenknecht, The Movies in the Age of Innocence
Martin Williams, Griffith: First Artist of the Movies

EARLY SOUND
Harry Geduld, The Birth of the Talkies
Alexander Walker, The Shattered Silents

1930's
Andrew Bergman, We're in the Money: Depression American and its
    Films
Roger Dooley, From Scarface to Scarlett: American Films in the
    1930's
Jeffrey Paine, The Simplification of American Life: Hollywood
    Films of the 1930's
Eugene Rosow, Born to Lose: The Gangster Film in America
Jack Shadoian, Dreams and Dead Ends: The American Gangster/Crime
    Film

1940's
Barbara Deming, Running Away From Myself

Pauline Kael, The Citizen Kane Book
Joseph McBride, Orson Welles
Hortense Powdermaker, Hollywood: The Dream Factory
Colin Shindler, Hollywood Goes to War, 1939-1952
Carlos Williams, The Dream Beside Me: The Movies and Children of
    the Forties

1950's
Herbert Biberman, Salt of the Earth
Larry Ceplair and Stephen Englund, The Inquisition in Hollywood
Lester Cole, Hollywood Red
Nora Sayre, Running Time: Films of the Cold War
Nancy Schwartz, The Hollywood Writers Wars

WOMEN IN FILM
Melva J. Baker, Images of Women in Film, 1941-1945
Patricia Erens, Sexual Strategems: The World of Women in Film
Sumiko Higashi, Virgins, Vamps, and Flappers: The American Silent
    Movie Heroine
Karen Kay and Gerald Peary, eds., Women and the Cinema
Joan Mellen, Big Bad Wolves: Masculinity in the American Film
Marjorie Rosen, Popcorn Venus

DOCUMENTARY
William Alexander, Film on the Left
Russel Campbell, Cinema Strikes Back
Raymond Fielding, The American Newsreel
_____, The March of Time
Lewis Jacobs, The Documentary Tradition
Bill Nichols, Newsreel: Documentary Filmaking and the American
    Left

WESTERNS
Kevin Brownlow, The War, the West, and the Wilderness
Jenni Calder, There Must Be a Lone Ranger
George Fenin and William K. Everson, The Western
John Lenihan, Showdown
Jack Nachbar, ed., Focus on the Western
Will Wright, Six Guns and Society

MINORITIES AND STEREOTYPING
Gretchen Bataille and Charles Silot, The Pretend Indians
Thomas Cripps, Slow Fade to Black
Ralph and Natasha Friar, The Only Good Indian
Daniel Leab, From Sambo to Superspade
Gerald Mapp, Blacks in American Film
John O'Connor, The Hollywood Indian
Allen Woll, The Latin Image in American Film

INDEPENDENT CINEMA
Jonas Mekas, Movie Journal: The Rise of the New American Cinema,
    1959-1971
P. Adams Sitney, Visionary Film
Amos Vogel, Film As a Subversive Art
Gene Youngblood, Expanded Cinema

A&S 3031
Louisiana State University
Selected Topics in Mass Media and American Society, 1938 to Present

D. H. Culbert   Fall Term 1975

September 3--Organizational Meeting

September 8--Recorded Broadcast: Orson Welles, "War of the Worlds"

I.   September 10--DISCUSS: Cantril, The Invasion From Mars, ix-xvi,
     3-222. Total: 226 pgs.

II. September 17--Recorded Broadcasts: Edward R. Murrow in London
     DISCUSS: Stott, Documentary Expression and Thirties America,
     75-91, copies on closed reserve [CR]; Culbert, News for
     Everyman, Introduction, chapter on Murrow, Conclusion, CR.
     Total: appx. 100 pgs.

     September 22--Film: Frank Capra, "The Battle of Britain"

III. September 24--DISCUSS: Glatzer and Raeburn, Frank Capra, 149-56,CR;
     Stouffer, The American Soldier, Vol. I, vii-ix, 3-5, 20-2, 51-9;
     Vol. III, 3-50, 247-79, CR; Ellul, Propaganda, v-xvii, 250-
     302, 3-87. Total: 249 pgs.

IV. October 1--DISCUSS: McLuhan, Understanding Media, vii-xi, 23-51,
     145-9, 155-61, 169-93, 248-94, 300-11; Stearns, McLuhan: Hot
     & Cool, 219-25, CR; Boorstin, "From News Gathering to News-
     making," 379-402, CR; Lasswell, "The Structure and Function
     of Communication in Society," 178-90, CR. Total: 176 pgs.

     October 6--Film: Erik Barnouw, "Hiroshima"

V.   October 8--DISCUSS: Hersey, Hiroshima, 1-116; Lifton, Death
     in Life, 3-56, 479-541. Total: 231 pgs.

VI. October 15--MIDTERM EXAM DUE. You are to prepare an analytical
     book review in approximately seven pages, typewritten and
     double-spaced, of Swanberg, Luce and His Empire, 15-400,
     666-7, 710-11. Total: 391 pgs. You must also look at
     five consecutive issues of Life or Time for a topic discussed
     in Swanberg's book.

     October 20--Lecture on development of television

VII. October 22--DISCUSS: Koen, The China Lobby, ix-xvii, 3-217;
     Key, "Pressure Groups," in Public Opinion and American
     Democracy, 500-31. Total: 253 pgs.

     October 27--Television videotape: Longines-Wittenauer "Chrono-
     scope" interview with Joseph R. McCarthy, Nov. 16, 1951;
     recorded audio for Murrow's "See It Now" program on McCarthy,
     March 9, 1954, and McCarthy rebuttal, April 6, 1954

VIII.   October 29--DISCUSS: Griffith, Politics of Fear, i-ii, 1-15,
        27-51, 243-70, 318-20; DeAntonio and Talbot, Point of
        Order, 5-108; Kendrick, Prime Time, 35-71; Murrow, "Address
        to Radio and Television Directors," all CR. Total: 217 pgs.

IX.   November 5--DISCUSS: Schneir, Invitation to an Inquest:
        Reopening the Rosenberg 'Atom Spy' Case, ix-xviii, 1-212,
        237-59, 397-403. Total: 248 pgs.

X.   November 12--DISCUSS: White and Abel, The Funnies, 1-38,
        179-89, CR; Berger, The Comic-Stripped American, 5-225.
        Total: 268 easy pages.

        November 17--Television videotape: Agnew speech, Nov. 13, 1969,
        plus additional television coverage

XI.   November 19--DISCUSS: Epstein, News From Nowhere, xi-xviii,
        3-25, 78-273. Total: 224 pgs.

XII.   November 26 (or 24)--DISCUSS: Lafever, TV and National
        Defense, v-viii, 1-167; CBS Response to Lafever, CR;
        Arlen, Living Room War, 18-22, 62-8, 79-84, 102-49,
        170-7, 201-6. Total: 244 pgs.

XIII.   December 3--DISCUSS: Fishwick, Popular Culture and the New
        Journalism (if published in time); Arlen, "Notes on the
        New Journalism,CR; Wilensky, "Mass Society and Mass Culture,"
        CR. Total: appx. 220 pgs.

XIV.   FINAL EXAM. You are to prepare a typewritten study of Television's
        impact on your own family in which you interview your own
        parents and grandparents as well as record your own memories.
        When was the first set purchased? What impact, if any, did
        television have on family structure? On your own education?
        Did family members see television programs before a set was
        purchased and if so, how? I am particularly interested in
        the late 1940s and early 1950s but feel free to discuss the
        recent past as well.

        Note: The following books, in paperback, are required for
                this course:

        Cantril, Invasion From Mars
        Ellul, Propaganda
        McLuhan, Understanding Media
        Hersey, Hiroshima
        Swanberg, Luce and His Empire
        Koen, The China Lobby
        Schneir, Invitation to an Inquest
        Berger, The Comic-Stripped American
        Epstein, News From Nowhere
        Lafever, TV and National Defense
        Arlen, Living Room War
        Fishwick, Popular Culture and the New Journalism

Senior Seminar   Fall, 1980
Popular Movements: 20th   Bruce Laurie
  Century America

The following books may be purchased at the Logos Bookstore in Amherst:

Karl Marx, Communist Manifesto
Raymond Williams, Marxism and Literature
Antonio Gramsci, Prison Notebooks
Harold Baron, The Demand for Black Labor
Zillah Eisenstein, Capitalist Patriarchy and the Case for Socialist Feminist
James Weinstein, Ambiguous Legacy
John Diggins, Up From Communism
Richard Cloward and Frances Piven, Poor People's Movements (recommended)
Mary Ryan, Womanhood in America (recommended)
Werner Sombart, Why is There No Socialism in the United States? (recommended)
Lucio Colletti, From Rousseau to Lenin (recommended)

These books and those marked with an asterisk below are on reserve in the Goodell
Library.

Sept. 4:   Introduction and Assignment of Papers

Sept. 9, 11, 16: Theory: Culture and Hegemony
            Reading: Marx, Communist Manifesto
                      Williams, Marxism, 75-141
                      *   "   , "Hegemony" in Keywords
                      Gramsci, Prison Notebooks, 55-60, 102-20, 381-472

            Suggested: Zygmunt Bauman, Culture as Praxis
                        P. Friedlander, The Emergence of a U.A.W. Local, 1936-
                        1939, Introduction
                        E.O. Wright, Class, Crisis, and the State
                        R. Cloward and F. Pivan, Poor People's Movements, 1-30

Sept. 18-23: Patriarchy and Race
            Reading: *H. Baron, Demand for Black Labor
                      Eisenstein, Capitalist Patriarchy, 1-106

            Suggested: J. Boggs, The American Revolution
                        J. Leggett, Race, Class, and Political Consciousness
                        C. Interrante and C. Lasser, "Victims of the Songs They
                        Sing: A Critique of Recent Work on Patriarchical
                        Culture and the Social Reconstruction of Gender,"
                        Radical History Review, (Spring-Summer 1979).
                        Ann Popkin, "The Personal is Political," in D. Cluster,
                        ed., They Should Have Served That Second Cup of Coffee
                        Ann Ferguson, "Women as a New Revolutionary Class in the
                        United States," in P. Walker, ed., Between Labor and
                        Capital

Sept. 25:   Open Date

168

Sept. 30 - Oct. 2: American Socialism
        Reading: Weinstein, Ambiguous Legacy, 1-25
                Sombart, Why there is No Socialism

      Paper I: The Sources and Practice of Socialist Culture

      J. Green, Grass-Roots Socialism
      J. Weinstein, Decline of Socialism in America, 1912-1925
    *D. Montgomery, Workers' Control in America, 48-90
      I.. Howe, World of our Fathers, 225-324
      M. Buhle, "Women in the Socialist Party, 1900-1914," Radical
         America, pamphlet
      P. Foner, "The Socialist Party and Socialist Women," in Foner,
         Women and the American Labor Movement
      B. Dancis, "Socialism and Women in the United States, 1900-1917,"
         Socialist Revolution (Jan.-Mar., 1976)
      J. Laslett, Labor and the Left
      Neil K. Basen, "Kate Richards O'Hare: The First Lady of American
         Socialism," LH, 21 (Spring 1980)

      Paper II: The Industrial Workers of the World

      M. Dubofsky, We Shall Be All
      L. DeCaux, Living Spirit of the Wobbies
      P. Foner, The Industrial Workers of the World, 1905-1917
      J. Kornbluh, Rebel Voices
      Mother Mary Jones, Autobiography of Mother Jones
      E.G. Flynn, Rebel Girl
      B. Jameson, "Imperfect Unions: Class and Gender in Cripple Creek,
         1894-1904," in W.D. Haywood, Autobiography

      Paper III: The Antisocialist Forces in America

      J. Laslett, "Reflections on the Failure of Socialism within the
         American Federation of Labor," Miss. Vall. Hist, Rev., 50 (March, 1966)
      M. Carson, American Labor Unions and Politics, 1900-1918
      J. Laslett and S.M. Lipsett, Failure of a Dream?
      J. Weinstein, The Corporate Ideal in the Liberal State, 1900-1918
    *D. Montgomery, Workers' Control in America, 48-90
      J. Weinstein, Decline of Socialism in America, 1912-1925
      I. Kipnis, The American Socialist Movement, 1895-1912
      C. Lasch, Agony of the American Left, 35-69
      P. Buhle, "Debsian Socialism and the New Immigrant Worker," in
         W. O'Neill, ed., Insights and Parallels

Oct. 7-9: Early 20th Century Feminism

      Reading: A. Kessler-Harris, "Where are the Organized Women Workers?"
               in N. Cott and L. Pleck, eds., A Heritage of Her Own
              L. Gordon, "Birth Control and Social Revolution," ibid

Paper I: Suffragists and Radicals

A. Kraditor, The Ideas of the Woman Suffrage Movement
L. Gordon, Woman's Body, Man's Right: A Social History of Birth
   Control in America
A. Wolfe, "Women, Consumerism, and the National Consumers' League,"
   Labor History, 16 (Summer 1975)
R. Jensen, "Family, Career, and Reform: Women Leaders in the
   Progressive Era," in D. Gordon, ed., The American Family in Social
   Historical Perspective
M. Sanger, My Fight for Birth Control
   _____, Women and the New Race
Florence Kelley, Once Upon a Time and Today
D. Cook, Female Support Networks and Political Activism," in Pleck
   and Cott, Heritage
W. O'Neill, Everyone Was Brave

Paper II: Workingwomen and their Allies

P. Foner, Women and the American Labor Movement, 290-391
Nancy S. Dye, "Creating a Feminist Alliance: Sisterhood and Class
   Conflict in the New York Women's Trade Union League, 1903-1914,"
   in Cantor and Laurie, eds., Class, Sex, and the Woman Worker
Robin M. Jacoby, "The Women's Trade Union League and American
   Feminism," ibid
Leslie Tentler, Wage-Earning Women
Virginia Y. McLaughlin, Family and Community: Italian Immigrants
   in Buffalo, New York, 1880-1930
Tamara Hareven and Randolph Langenbach, Amoskeag
   _____, "The Laborers of Manchester New Hampshire, 1912-1922:
   The Role of Family and Ethnicity in Adjustment to Industrial Life,"
   Labor History, 16 (Summer 1975)
J. Bodnar, "Immigration and Modernization: The Case of Slavic
   Peasants in Industrial America," Journal of Social History, 9 (1975)
Judith E. Smith, "Our Own Kind: Family and Community Networks,"
   Radical History Review, 17 (Spring 1978)
I. Howe, World of our Fathers, 265-70
A. Kessler-Harris, "Organizing the Unorganizable: Three Jewish
   Women and their Union," in Cantor and Laurie, eds., Class, Sex, and
   the Woman Worker
M. Byington, Homestead: The Households of a Mill Town

Oct. 14-16: Black Workers and Their Leaders
      Reading: *A. Meier, "Negro Class Structure and Ideology in the
                  Age of Booker T. Washington," Phylon, 22 (Fall 1962),
                  258-66
                *W. Tuttle, "Labor Militancy and Racial Violence: The
                  Black Worker in Chicago, 1894-1919," Labor History, 10
                  (Summer 1969)
                Weinstein, 87-92

Paper I: From Washington to Garvey

Booker T. Washington, Up from Slavery
W.E.B. DuBois, Souls of Black Folk
A. Meier, Negro Thought in America, 1880-1915
E. David Cronin, Black Moses

170

Tony Martin, Race First
Theodore Vincent, Black Power and the Garvey Movement
J. Anderson, A. Philip Randolph
Ernest Allen, "Marcus Garvey and Booker T. Washington: Patterns of
    Militancy and Accomodation" (mimeo)
E. Tolbert, "Outpost Garveyism and the U.N.I.A. Rank and File,"
    Journal of Black Studies, 5 (March 1975)
B.J. Ross, J.E. Spingern and the Rise of the N.A.A.C.P.
T.J. Heiting, W.E.B. DuBois and the Development of Pan-Africanism

Paper II: Black Workers and Black Communities

K. Kusmer, A Ghetto Takes Shape: Black Cleveland, 1870-1930
A. Spear, Black Chicago: The Making of a Ghetto, 1890-1920
G. Osofsky, Harlem: The Making of a Ghetto
F. Henri, The Great Migration
D. Katzman, Seven Days a Week
P. Foner, Organized Labor and the Black Worker, 64-143
E. Rudwick, Race Riot at East St. Louis
J. Bodnar, "The Impact of the 'New Immigration' on the Black Worker:
    Steelton Pa., 1880-1920," Labor History 17 (Spring 1976)
P.W. Worthman, "Working-Class Mobility in Bermingham, Ala., 1880-
    1914," in T. Hareven, ed., Anonymous Americans

Oct. 21-23: American Communism: The Early Years

    Reading: Weinstein, Ambiguous Legacy, 26-56
             *J. Brecher, Strike! ch. 4

Paper I: An Analysis of Leninism

I. Colletti, Rosseau to Lenin, 45-108
V.I. Lenin, What is to Be Done
_____, Left-Wing Communism
_____, State and Revolution
Moshe Lewin, Lenin's Last Struggle
T. Draper, American Communism and Soviet Russia

Paper II: A New Hegemony

S. Ewen, Captains of Consciousness
R. and H. Lynd, Middletown
L. Tilly and J. Scott, Women, Work and the Family, 176-213
M. Hillard, "New Immigrants in the Formation of the American Working
    Class: The Case of Chicago, 1900-1930" (mimeo)
Joann Vanek, "Time Spent in Housework," in Cott and Pleck, eds.,
    Heritage
F. Stricker, "Cookbooks and Law Books," ibid
M. Davies, "Woman's Place is at the Typewriter," Radical America, 3
    (July-August 1974)
L. Pruette, Women and Leisure: A Study of Social Waste
W. O'Neill, Everyone was Brave, 225-94

Oct. 28-30: The Thirties and Lost Opportunities

      Reading: Weinstein, Ambiguous Legacy, 57-86
           *J. Brecher, Strike! ch. 5

      Paper I: Communism and Worker Militancy

      H. Haywood, Black Bolshevik
      A. Richmond, Long View from the Left
      G. Charney, A Long Journey
      Joseph Starobin, American Communism in Crisis, 20-47
      Bert Cochran, Labor and Communism
      *P. Friedlander, The Emergence of a U.A.W. Local, 1936-1939
      Sharon Strom, "'We're No Kitty Foyles': Organizing Office Workers
        for the CIO," (mimeo)
      P. Foner, Organized Labor and the Black Worker, 188-237
      S. Lynd, "The Possibility of Radicalism in the Early 1930s: The
        Case of Steel," Radical America, 6 (Nov.-Dec., 1972)
      J. Gree, "Working-Class Militancy in the Depression," RA, 6
        (Nov.-Dec. 1972)

      Paper II: The New State, The New Party

      D. Montgomery, Workers' Control in America, 153-80
      C. Klare, "The Deradicalization of the Wagner Act and the Origins
        of Modern Legal Consciousness," Minn. Law Rev., 62 (1978)
      K. Kolko, Main Currents in Modern American History, 100-56
      D. Potter and W. Goetzmann, The New Deal and Unemployment
      Barton J. Bernstein, "The New Deal and the Conservative Achievements
        of Liberal Reform," in Bernstein, ed., Towards a New Past
      St. Clare Drake and H. Clayton, Black Metropolis, 342-77
      S. Lubell, Future of American Politics, ch. 3
      I. Bernstein, Turbulent Years, 172-351
      R. Hurd, "New Deal Labor Policy and the Containment of Radical Union
        Activity," Journal of Radical Political Econ., 8 (Fall 1976)

Nov. 4-6: Hot War, Cold War

      Reading: Weinstein, Ambiguous Legacy, 93-113
           *D. Oshinsky, "Labor's Cold War," in Griffith and
              Theoharis, eds., The Specter
           *J. Green, "Fighting on two Fronts: Working-Class
              Militancy in the 1940s," Radical America, 9 (July-Aug. 1975)

      Paper I: Race, Sex, and the Unions in Wartime

      J. Seidman, American Labor from Defense to Reconversion
      "Rosie the Riveter," etc., Radical America, ibid
      J.E. Trey, "Women in the War Economy," Rev. of Radical Political
        Economics, 10 (July, 1978)
      R. Milkman, "Women's Work and the Economic Crisis," in Cott and
        Pleck, Heritage
      Mary P. Ryan, Womanhood in America, 187-218

Donald Critchlow, "Communist Unions and Racism: A Comparative
Study of the Responses of the U.E. and N.M.U. to the Black
Question during World War II," Labor History, 17 (Spring 1976)
W. Chafe, The American Woman, 135-95
A. Meier and E. Rudwick, Black Detroit and the Rise of the U.A.W.
P. Foner, Organized Labor and the Black Worker, 238-68
H. Garfinkel, When Negroes March
C. Denby, Indignant Heart, 1-179
H. Sitkoff, "Racial Militancy and Interracial Violence during
World War II," Journal of American History (Dec. 1971)
Sumner Rosen, "The CIO Era, 1935-1955," in Juliun Jacobsen, ed.,
The Negro and the American Labor Movement

Paper II: The Cold War and Organized Labor

Mary McAuliffe, Crisis on the Left
Lawrence Ladler, Power on the Left, 19-102
R. Griffith and A. Theoharis, eds., The Specter
B. Cochran, Labor and Communism
F. Marquart, An Automobile Worker's Journal
D. Caute, The Great Fear
Len DeCaux, Labor Radical, 470-545
R. Radosh, American Labor and U.S. Foreign Policy

Nov. 11-13: Blacks in Postwar America

Reading: *W. Wilson, The Declining Significance of Race

Paper I: The Black Reserve Army, Protest, and the State

R. Edwards, Contested Terrain, chs. 9-10
K. Marx, Capital, I, sec. 3 of "The General Law of Capitalist
Accumulation"
Michael Poire, "Manpower Policy," in S. Beer and S. Barringer, The
State and the Poor
_____, "Notes for a Theory of Labor Market Stratificaion,"
in R. Edwards, et al., eds., Labor Market Segmentation
Cloward and Piven, Regulating the Poor
_____, Poor People's Movements, 264-361
T. Hershberg, et al., "A Tale of Three Cities," (mimeo)
U.S. President's Advisory Commission on Civil Disorders, Report
T. Lowi, End of Liberalism, 167-268
R. Allen, Black Awakening in Capitalist America, 193-245

Paper II: The Civil Rights Movement: A Critique

W. Wilson, The Declining Significance of Race
Cloward and Piven, Poor People's Movements, 181-263
R. Allen, Black Awakening in Capitalist America, 1-192
L. Killian and C. Smith, "Negro Protest Leaders in a Southern
Community," Social Forces, 38 (March 1960)

173

Martin Luther King, Jr., Why We Can't Wait
_____, Stride toward Freedom
Lewis Lomax, The Negro Revolt
J.R. Gusfield, Protest, Reform, and Revolt
Jack. L. Walker, "The Functions of Disunity: Negro Leadership in
a Southern City," Journal of Negro Education (Summer, 1963)
A. Meier and E. Rudwick, CORE

Nov. 18-20: The New Left and Partyless Radicalism

Reading: Weinstein, Ambiguous Legacy, 114-59
          *M. Teodori, ed., The New Left, 163-72

Paper: The New Left: A Critique

Weinstein, Ambiguous Legacy, 114-50
K. Sale, S.D.S.
R.E. Flacks, "The Liberated Generation: An Exploration of the Roots
of Student protest," Journal of Soc. Issues, 3 (1967)
K. Cenistou, Young Radicals: Notes on Committed Youth
H. Zinn, The New Abolitionists
M. Cantor, The Divided Left, 182-227
M. Teodori, The New Left (ed.)
James Foreman, The Making of Black Revolutionaries
S. Carmichael and C. Hamilton, Black Power
R. Allen, Black Awakening in Capitalist America, 246-73
J. O'Brien, "The New Left, 1960-1965," Radical America (May-June 1968;
"The New Left, 1965-1967," ibid) (Sept.-Oct. 1976; "The New Left,
1967-1968," ibid., Nov.-Dec. 1968)
George Vickers, The Formation of the New Left: The Early Years
C. Lasch, Agony of the American Left, 117-212

Nov. 25-Dec. 2: The New Feminisms

Reading: W. Chafe, *Women and Equality

Paper: Structural Origins of the New Feminism

L. Gordon, "The Struggle for Reproductive Freedom," in Eisentein,
Capitalist Patriarchy
Mary P. Ryan, Womanhood in America, 183-245
J. Freeman, "The Origins of the Women's Liberation Movement," Am.
Jour. of Soc., 78 #Jan. 1973)
Tauber and Sweet, "Family and Work: The Social Life cycle of Women,"
in J. Kreps, Women in the American Economy
J. Kreps and R. Clark, Age, Sex, and Work
P.J. Andrisani, "Job Statification among Working Women," Signs, 3
(Spring 1978)
H. Braverman, Labor and Monopoly Capital, 293-373
L. Tilly and J. Scott, Women, Work and Family, 214-32
J. Neipert Hedges, and J.K. Barnett, "Working Women and the Division
of Household Tasks," Monthly Labor Rev. (Apr. 1972)

Fall, 1982   Michael Zuckerman
HISTORY 373
Splitting: The 1960s in America

WEE HOURS -

William H. Whyte, The Organization Man, ch. 1, 2, 6, 9, 10, 14,
   16, 23, 26, 28
Evan Connell, Mrs. Bridge
Daniel Bell, The End of Ideology, pp. 393-407

FALSE DAWN -

Dwight Eisenhower, "Farewell Radio and Television Address to the
   American People," Public Papers of the Presidents of the United
   States, Eisenhower, 1960-61, pp. 1035-40
Sidney Kraus, ed., The Great Debates, pp. 348-430
John Kennedy, "Inaugural Address," Public Papers of the Presidents:
   Kennedy, 1961, pp. 1-3
David Halberstam, The Best and the Brightest, ch. 1-4
Tom Wolfe, The Right Stuff, ch. 1-6, 9-10, epilogue

DAYBREAK -

David Welch, "In the Shadow of Dallas," Ramparts (November, 1966)
"Playboy Interview: Jim Garrison," Playboy 14 (October, 1967), 59ff.
Josiah Thompson, "The Crossfire that Killed President Kennedy,"
   Saturday Evening Post 240 (December 2, 1967), 27ff.
Ralph Nader, "The Corvair Story," The Nation 201 (November 1,
   1965), 295-301
Martin Luther King, "Letter from Birmingham Jail," in Why We Can't
   Wait
Martin Luther King, "I have a Dream," New York Times, August 29,
   1963, p. 21
Ann Moody, Coming of Age in Mississippi, parts 2 and 4
Students for a Democratic Society, Port Huron Statement (on re-
   serve)
Sara Davidson, Loose Change, parts I and II
Most anything by Bob Dylan, the Beatles, and/or the Rolling Stones
   from the early or mid-sixties

BLOWIN' IN THE WIND -

Doris Kearns, LBJ and the American Dream
Adam Smith, The Money Game, ch. 1, 3, 7, 8, 10-13, 15
Jules billard, "The Revolution in American Agriculture," National
   Geographic (February, 1970), 147-85
Jerry Kramer, Instant Replay, ch. 1-3
Barbara Garson, All the Livelong Day, pp. 1-21, 73-126, 140-56
Leonard Lewin, Report from Iron Mountain
Tony Sanchez, The Rolling Stones, ch. 1-7, 18, 25
Sara Davidson, Loose Change, part III
Philip Slater, The Pursuit of Loneliness
Michael Herr, Dispatches, pp. 13-67, 81-147
Susan Sontag, "Trip to Hanoi," in Styles of Radical Will

HIGH NOON -

    James Baldwin, The Fire Next Time
    Norman Podhoretz, "My Negro Problem - and Ours," Commentary 35
       (1968), 93-101
    Norman Mailer, Miami and the Siege of Chicago, part 2
    Charles Reich, "Reflections: The Limits of Duty," New Yorker
       (June 19, 1971), 52-7

INTO THE SUNSET -

    Hunter Thompson, Fear and Loathing in Las Vegas
    Sara Davidson, Loose Change, part IV
    Marshall Frady, Wallace, parts 1 and 4
    Michael Rogin and John Shover, Political Change in California,
       ch. 6
    Robert Lifton, "Protean Man," Partisan Review (winter, 1968),
       13-27

The American Radical Tradition

NEH Summer Seminar   1982
Professor E. Foner

(Books marked with an asterisk are in print in paperback and
available at Barnes and Noble Bookstore, Fifth Avenue and
18th Street, New York City)

Schedule of Sessions

1. (June 22): Introductory Session

2. (June 24): Viewing the Tradition

        Aileen Kraditor, "American Radical Historians on
            Their Heritage", Past and Present, 56, August,
            1972, 136-53
        James Green, "Reply to Kraditor"; Past and Present,
            69, November 1975, 122-31
        Seymour M. Lipset, "Why No Socialism in the United States",
            in Seweryn Bialer and Sophia Sluzer, eds., Sources
            of Contemporary Radicalism, 31-149
        Raymond Williams, "Base and Superstructure in Marxist
            Cultural Theory", New Left Review, Nov. - Dec.,
            1973, 3-16
        *Aileen Kraditor, The Radical Persuasion, 1890-1917,
            chs. 2-3

3. (June 29): Origins of American Radicalism

        E.P. Thompson, The Making of the English Working Class,
            Pt. I
        Jesse Lemisch, "Jack Tar in the Streets", William and
            Mary Quarterly, XXV, October, 1968
        *Alfred Young, ed., The American Revolution, 3-35, 125-57

4. (July 1): The American Revolution and American Radicalism

        *Eric Foner, Tom Paine and Revolutionary America
        *Alfred Young, ed., The American Revolution, 233-72, 447-61
        J.G.A. Pocock, The Machiavellian Moment, ch. 15

5. (July 6): The Early Labor Movement

        *Alan Dawley, Class and Community
        David Montgomery, "The Shuttle and the Cross: Weavers
            and Artisans in the Kensington Riots of 1844",
            Journal of Social History, VI, Summer, 1972, 411-46
        Edward Pessen, "The Workingmen's Parties Revisited",
            Labor History, IV, Fall, 1963, 203-26
        Friedrich Lenger, "Class, Culture, and Class Consciousness
            in Ante-Bellum Lynn", Social History, VI, October,
            1981, 317-32

6. (July 8): The Origins of Feminism

>*Ellen DuBois, Feminism and Suffrage
Berenice A. Carroll, Liberating Women's History, 75-92,
278-300, 330-34, 385-99
Carol Smith-Rosenberg, "Beauty, the Beast, and the
Militant Women", American Quarterly, October, 1971
562-84
Thomas Dublin, "Women, Work and Protest in the E'rly
Lowell Mills", Labor History, XVI, Winter, 1975
99-116
Joan Kelly, "The Doubled Vision of Feminist Theory",
Feminist Studies, V, Spring, 1979, 216-27

7. (July 13): Slavery and Abolition

Lewis Perry and Michael Fellman, eds., Anti-Slavery
Reconsidered, VII-XVI, 3-23, 195-218
Aileen Kraditor, Means and Ends in American Abolitionism,
chs. 2-5, 8
John Thomas, "Romantic Reform in America", American
Quarterly, December, 1965, 656-81
David Donald, Lincoln Reconsidered, ch. 2
*Eric Foner, Politics and Ideology in the Age of he Civil
War, ch. 4

8. (July 15): The Civil War and American Radicalism

*David Montgomery, Beyond Equality, chs. 1-6
*Eric Foner, Politics and Ideology in the Age of the Civil
War, chs. 6-7

9. (July 20): Race, Class, and Radicalism in the Gilded Age

*Herbert Gutman, Work, Culture, and Society in Industrializing
America, chs. 1-3, 5
Leon Fink, "Class Conflict in the Gilded Age: The Figure
and the Phantom", Radical History Review, Fall-Winter
1975, 74-90
John R. Thomasm "Utopia for an Urban Age", Perspectives
In American History, VI, 1972, 135-66
*Eric Foner, Politics and Ideology in the Age of the Civil
War, ch. 8
David Montgomery, "Labor and the Republic in Industrial
America, 1860-1920", Mouvement Social, 111, April-
June, 1980, 210-15

10. (July 23): <u>Populism</u>

        *Lawrence Goodwyn, <u>The Populist Moment in America</u>
        *Richard Hofstadter, <u>The Age of Reform</u>, pts. I-III
        Chester McA. Destler, "Western Radicalism 1865-1901,"
           <u>Mississippi Valley Historical Review</u>, December
           1944, 335-68

11. (July 27): <u>American Socialism</u>

        *Melvyn Dubofsky, <u>We Shall Be All</u>, chs. 4-11
        Charles Leinenweber, "Socialists in the Streets,"
           <u>Science and Society</u>, XLI, 1977, 152-71
        *James Green, <u>Grass-Roots Socialism</u>, chs. 1, 3-4, 6
        Mari Jo Buhle, "Women and the Socialist Party,
           1901-1914," <u>Radical America</u>, IV, Feb, 1970, 36-58
        *Aileen Kraditor, <u>The Radical Persuasion</u>
           <u>1890-1917</u>, chs. 1, 5, 7

12. (July 29): <u>The Decline of Socialism</u>

        James Weinstein, <u>The Decline of Socialism in America</u>
        Paul Buhle, "Debsian Socialism and the 'New Immigrant'
           Worker," in William O'Neill, ed. <u>Insights and</u>
           <u>Parallels</u>, 249-304
        *James Green, <u>Grass-Roots Socialism</u>, chs. 7-9
        John Alt, "Beyond Class: The Decline of Industrial
           Labor and Leisure," <u>Telos</u>, XXVIII, Summer 1976, 55-80
        Eric Foner, "The Men and the Symbols: Sacco and Vanzetti
           <u>The Nation</u>, August 20-27, 1977, 135-40
        Estelle Freedman, "Separatism as Strategy: Female
           Institution Building and American Feminism, 1870-
           1930," <u>Feminist Studies</u>, V, Fall, 1979, 512-29

13. (August 3): <u>The Origins of Black Radicalism</u>

        *August Meier, <u>Negro Thought in America</u>, chs. 1, 7-11, 14
        Theodore Vincent, <u>Black Power and the Garvey Movement</u>,
           chs. 1-7
        William Tuttle, "Labor Conflict and Racial Violence:
           The Black Worker in Chicago, 1894-1919,"
           <u>Labor History</u>, X, 1969, 408-32
        Neil Betten and Raymond Mohl, "The Evolution of Racism
           in an Industrial City," <u>Journal of Negro History</u>,
        Manning Marable, "A. Philip Randolph and the
           Foundations of Black American Socialism,"
           <u>Radical America</u>, XIV, March-April 1980, 7-32

14. (August 5): The 'Old Left'

    *Joseph Starobin, American Communism in Crisis, chs. 1-2
    Mark Naison, "Harlem Communists and the Politics
        of Black Protest," Marxist Perspectives, 3, Fall
        1978, 20-51
    Roger Keeran, "Everything for Victory: Communist
        Influence in the Auto Industry During World War II,"
        Science and Society, XLIII, Spring, 1979, 1-28
    Max Gordon, "The Communist Party of the 1930's and
        the New Left," Socialist Revolution, 27,
        Jan-March, 1976, 11-66
    Mike Davis, "The Barren Marriage of American Labor and
        the Democratic Party," New Left Review, 124,
        Nov-Dec 1980, 43-84

15. (August 10): The 'New Left'

    *Sara Evans, Personal Politics
    *Peter Clecak, Radical Paradoxes, chs. 1-2, 6-7
    *Robert Allen, Black Awakening in Capitalist America,
        chs. 1-4

16. (August 12): American Radicalism Today

    Harry C. Boyte, "Populism and the Left," Democracy,
        May, 1981, 53-66
    Barbara Haber, "Is Personal Life Still a Political
        Issue?" Feminist Studies, V, Fall, 1979, 417-31
    Current issues of: In These Times, Daily World,
        The Guardian, The Militant, Womanews

TABLE OF CONTENTS

VOLUME I

INTRODUCTION

WOMEN'S HISTORY

A. SURVEY COURSES

C. ETHNIC WOMEN'S HISTORY – AFRO-AMERICAN AND CHICANO

D. WOMEN AND RELIGION

E. WOMEN AND EDUCATION

F. SOCIAL HISTORY, WOMEN AND WORK

G. THEORY AND METHODOLOGY

Documents have been reproduced from the originals as submitted.